CAD/CAM
APPLICATIONS FOR BUSINESS

CAD/CAM
APPLICATIONS FOR BUSINESS

by Stuart W. Hubbard

ORYX PRESS
1985

The rare Arabian Oryx is believed to have inspired the myth of the unicorn. This desert antelope became virtually extinct in the early 1960s. At that time several groups of international conservationists arranged to have a group of animals sent to the Phoenix Zoo to be the nucleus of a captive breeding herd. Today the Oryx population is over 400 and herds have been returned to reserves in Israel, Jordan, and Oman.

Copyright © 1985 by
The Oryx Press
2214 North Central at Encanto
Phoenix, AZ 85004-1483

Published simultaneously in Canada

Printed and Bound in the United States of America

Library of Congress Cataloging in Publication Data

Hubbard, Stuart W.
    CAD/CAM: applications for business.

    Bibliography: P.
    Includes index.
    1. CAD/CAM systems.   I. Title.
TS 155.6.H83   1985   670.42'7   85-3074
ISBN 0-89774-167-6

To Linda Wanek Hubbard
this book is dedicated
with sincerest respect and affection

Table of Contents

Preface   ix

Introduction   xiii

Chapter 1: A Brief History   1
Chapter 2: The Viability of CAD/CAM Technology Today: Where It Is
                and What It Can Do   11
Chapter 3: Standard System Components   29
Chapter 4: Ergonomics   49
Chapter 5: System and Applications Software: Guidelines for
                Evaluation   57
Chapter 6: Personnel and Training   69
Chapter 7: Justification and Evaluation in Business   77
Chapter 8: System Management   87
Appendix I: The Use of Color   103
Appendix II: The Request for Proposal (RFP)   107

Glossary   113

Selected Bibliography   119

Index   123

Preface

This book advocates computer-aided design and computer-aided manufacturing (CAD/CAM) technology. CAD/CAM is a viable approach to many drafting, engineering, and production tasks.

The value of this technology has been demonstrated many times. In the most general sense, CAD/CAM needs no more justification. Nevertheless, in its application to specific production settings or to specific industries, and in its ability to remain consistent with financial plans or business agenda, CAD/CAM technology is likely to need a great deal of justification before it can be brought on-line. The following pages contain suggestions on how to prepare for that task.

I readily concede that CAD/CAM technology is not the answer to everyone's drafting or manufacturing needs. The purpose of this book is to provide sufficient information for business people, educators, and scientific researchers to determine for themselves whether CAD/CAM technology can be usefully and economically applied to their work.

Such determinations are not arrived at easily. Despite being based on sound and established technology, CAD/CAM systems remain expensive and complex; their implementation will be disruptive to the most stable working environment. Many considerations should be taken into account before the final decision is made. For instance, CAD/CAM systems may require specially trained personnel to run them, specially constructed rooms to house them, custom software to make them useful, and elaborate maintenance to keep them working. A great deal of sorting out must be done before anyone, even an expert, can decide whether one CAD/CAM system or, indeed, any available CAD/CAM system can be made to address the needs of a particular business, educational, or research setting in a way that is both economical and satisfactory to system users.

Such sorting out usually begins by defining and quantifying the data processing tasks that can be handled by a CAD/CAM system. Next, some methodology must be adopted for evaluating the CAD/CAM systems currently on the market. This methodology must be applied and the findings analyzed against a backdrop of budget limitations, available personnel, cost efficiency studies, maintenance requirements, site planning constraints, financing plans, system configuration options, and a host of other factors. Doing this analysis thoroughly and without error is a challenging undertaking at best. This book can help.

CAD/CAM: Applications for Business might also be well used as an introductory text to the CAD/CAM industry and its technology. As such, it is a useful adjunct to college courses in business, data processing, and engineering. It should be noted that CAD/CAM technology is itself sufficiently established and vital to be offered as a major field of study at many universities in this country and abroad. This book is a valuable asset to anyone pursuing such studies—or, for that matter, to anyone with an abiding interest in CAD/CAM.

Primarily, however, *CAD/CAM: Applications for Business* addresses the issues involved in the practical application of CAD/CAM technology and in its implementation. It answers such questions as: What are the standard components of a turnkey CAD/CAM system? How should the data base be organized? Against what criteria should a workstation be evaluated? Which industries stand to benefit most from CAD/CAM? Which peripheral devices are best for the input or output of what kind of graphics data? How should a centralized system be managed? A decentralized system? What is the best way to maintain such systems? To house them? To upgrade them? These are the kinds of important and unavoidable questions facing anyone contemplating the purchase of a CAD/CAM system or currently managing such a system. *CAD/CAM: Applications for Business* provides the means to some answers.

When reading this book for the first time, it is best to proceed straight through. The chapters are organized to build on one another, and reading them in consecutive order makes this organization more apparent and a first reading more successful. Nevertheless, each chapter concerns an independent topic and can be used for reference on specific subjects.

Lastly, let me remind all readers that the implementation of CAD/CAM is very difficult to do well. It takes patience, open-mindedness, careful planning, and persistence. Many departments will be asked to cooperate and to communicate on levels they are not used to. Management will be required get involved at the beginning and stay involved. Expectations must remain realistic. Training may take time. Nonetheless, given the right circumstances, CAD/CAM systems, when implemented well and maintained properly, are invaluable tools.

Stuart W. Hubbard
Boulder, CO

Introduction

Computer-aided design/computer-aided manufacturing (CAD/CAM) is difficult to define without being either too vague or too complex. A short, formal definition might run something like this: "CAD/CAM refers to the application of computer technology to any or all aspects of production from design through fabrication."

To be more complete, we could break it down a little further. CAD describes the use of computers to aid in the creation of schematics, blueprints, plots, and other drawings which are of sufficient accuracy to be used to guide the production of manufactured goods, components, or structures. These schematics, blueprints, etc. also imply an organized data base of pictorial information that can be used again and again according to the needs of various more specific design applications such as structural engineering, electrical schematics, piping design, or technical illustration.

CAM, on the other hand, describes the use of computers to produce data employed to assist in or control all or part of manufacturing processes. These processes include such things as numerically controlled machine tooling, parts programing, and robotics. Here again, the data imply an organization that, in this case, permits the automation of sophisticated analysis programs, engineering tasks, and finite element modeling processes among others. By putting the power of CAD and CAM together, industry has a formidable production tool that can not only add speed to most manufacturing tasks, but can make them more efficient, more accurate, and more versatile.

There is no easy way to be more (succinct) about what CAD/CAM means. It is a very complicated business. It is hard to get a firm handle on this technology, and most people end up getting thoroughly bogged down in tedious definitions and (incomprehensible jargon.)

But if we set the definitions aside for a moment and just look at the technology we can begin to see that the world of CAD/CAM is, at its roots, essentially visual. It consists of computers and the pictures they can draw. At that level it seems straightforward.

The complications come in the application of computer pictures to practical industrial problems. After all, when we say CAD/CAM is "visual," we imply many things. Creativity, for instance, is one such implication. And as much as anything, it is creativity that has given rise to the entire CAD/CAM industry. The ability to use computer pictures to create useful items— drawings, designs, illustrations—is what has spurred additional research and development in CAD/CAM. That research has not slowed.

When computer graphics began it was not immediately useful, but it was fun and it was interesting. Scientists saw that it had enormous potential. But for a long time computer graphics and CAD/CAM were regarded as illegitimate children of the data processing industry—toys that had not yet been applied usefully. Years of further development have proven otherwise; today CAD/ CAM is an integral part of modern drafting and manufacturing. Now we have a whole branch of computer science dedicated to computer-aided drafting and computer-aided manufacturing.

Creativity is still the driving force behind computer graphics. If it does nothing else, computer graphics extend our ability to create visual images easily and quickly. This extension is so remarkable, in fact, that to the uninitiated, CAD/CAM is almost magical. Even to the initiated, it is an awesome visual tool.

Extending Our Vision

Developing new tools is second nature to human beings. And one of the most important of all our new tools is the computer. The proof of that can be found by noting the myriad ways in which we have put computers to use.

CAD/CAM is just a small segment of the computer industry, but it is among the fastest growing. The potential for applying computers to manufacturing and drafting tasks is still not fully defined, let alone realized. The future of CAD/CAM is bound to be rich and various.

Using computers to produce and manipulate pictorial data augments our modern penchant for all things visual. Visual media are a powerful means for disseminating information, expressing ideas, advancing opinions. The Wharton School of Business conducted a study on the effects of using graphics in business meetings. The study revealed that meetings can be shortened as much as 28%, be more effective, and be more likely to produce a consensus when graphics are used. The findings showed that 67% of those present at meetings agreed with presentations when graphics were used as opposed to only 50% when graphics were not used.[1]

And, to further prove the point that graphics are powerful communications tools, one need only look at the proliferation of televisions, movie houses, billboards, the importance of logos and packaging, the value of photography and the visual arts. Computerizing graphic data is simply another way of extending the possibilities of visual communications.

CAD/CAM vs. Computer Graphics

To get at a precise understanding of what CAD/CAM is, we must also be aware of what it is not. It is valuable, therefore, before we begin to fall into a semantic tangle, to understand the meanings of and the differences between the terms "computer graphics" and "computer-aided design/computer-aided manufacturing." In common usage the terms are often synonomous. For the more precise purposes of this book, however, a distinction must be made between them.

"Computer graphics" is the more general term. It refers to that entire branch of computer science which deals with the creation or modification of pictorial data for any purpose. "Computer-aided design/computer-aided manufacturing," on the other hand, refers more specifically to the application of computer graphics to problems encountered in drafting or in the support of production processes. By extension, it also entails things beyond computer graphics, such as numerical control, group technology, and data base management.

More important, CAD/CAM also implies a technology in which there is interactivity between a person and a machine—that is, where the computer operator and computer system communicate in meaningful ways. This is a singularly important concept and it will underpin much of the discussion in this book. Wherever these terms are used in the ensuing chapters, the distinction is maintained.

The distinction is useful because it provides a convenient way to differentiate between 2 entirely different ways of thinking. Computer graphics is a generalized, multi-disciplined approach to creating any kind of image. CAD/CAM, on the other hand, is an ordered, comprehensive application of graphics technology to a specific task—product development. In either case, they are decidedly visual disciplines. A person and a machine work together manipulating lines and space and form and color and geometry and in doing so create something new.

The Power to Create

The power of CAD/CAM systems to create visual data is enormous, but it can be overstated. We must keep things in perspective—the real creativity in CAD/CAM, as in any discipline, remains in the minds of the people involved, in this case, the CAD/CAM system users. When the system displays graphics data on the screen or outputs them to a plotter, it is creating images of ideas that formed first in the mind of the operator. CAD/CAM is a tool, like any other, and we should remain realistic about what it can do for us.

What the graphics system operator sees on the workstation screen is not real; it is an image, a representation; it is a kind of sophisticated illusion. It is made real by the imagination of the person viewing it.

We say that a solid object exists on the screen. But it is not solid. We cannot touch it or lift it or taste it. It is a picture, a display of electronic data. It is a mathematical description of a solid object so complete that we can use that description to build an object exactly like the one we have described on the screen—exactly, and down to the smallest detail of color, density, size, and shape. Using the image as a guide, we can create a real object easier than if we were to start from scratch.

The leap from representation to reality is made CAM. This is the real value of CAD/CAM in economic terms. Many of the middle steps of traditional manufacturing are made obsolete. For instance, there is no need to create prototypes or to do extensive real world testing. There is no need to keep copies of large engineering drawings or to worry about obsolete data. There is no need to keep a separate system for bills of materials or to keep separate records of scrap materials or to conduct productivity surveys. All of these things are done automatically with CAD/CAM. The steps are not fewer, but they are automated and taken out of the hands of engineers and drafters who could better spend their time on the more creative aspects of their work.

CAD/CAM extends our vision and frees our minds of cluttering detail. And as the industry continues to evolve and as the technology becomes better and more sophisticated, CAD/CAM will move us into new areas of design, manufacturing, and art.

Reference

1. Al Tauber, "Driving Forces Lead to Explosive Growth," *Computer Graphics World* 10 (9) (September 1984): 70.

Chapter 1
A Brief History

The history of computer-aided drafting/computer-aided manufacturing (CAD/CAM) is longer and more varied than many people, even those who work with it, realize. The technology did not spring up magically overnight like a backyard mushroom.

The roots of CAD/CAM can be traced to the earliest computer-driven output devices. These devices—big, cumbersome, full of glowing vacuum tubes and crude mechanical parts—were originally devised in the early 1950s for the simple purpose of drawing or displaying points and straight lines. The images they produced were often symbolic rather than representational, depicting, for instance, the changing relation between 2 variables, such as time and speed, or velocity and direction, or earnings and revenues.

These early output devices, therefore, lent themselves naturally to such rote tasks as producing graphs or trend lines. The data could be determined easily enough by even the earliest computing systems. It was then sent to output devices over a few feet of coaxial cable. As graphics technology it was very rudimentary, limited as it was to output, but it was graphics just the same. Graphic input would come later, and with it, the beginnings of an interactive, symbiotic relation between human and machine that marked the genesis of CAD/CAM.

Yet the importance of drawing lines or points must not be discounted. Despite its relative simplicity, and despite our vantage point after more than 25 years of additional development effort, such drawing is undeniably useful—especially when representing data that are spatial or linear in nature. It is much easier to understand an illustration than a verbal or mathematical description of the same information.

We live in a predominantly visual world. Researchers realized this very early on. Even in the days of the most rudimentary forms of computer technology, graphics output devices were common peripheral equipment. For example, 2-dimensional ink plotters have been outputting graphics data for 30 years; so have on-line oscilloscopes and microfilm photographic plotters. Hundreds of these devices were in use long before the term computer-aided design/computer-aided manufacturing (CAD/CAM) was ever coined and before the idea of computer graphics became widely thought of as a viable computer application. In other words, despite the fact these activities may not always have been termed "computer graphics," graphic representation of computer data is not a new idea.

The First Graphics Output Devices

As far back as the early 1950s the Lincoln Laboratory at the Massachusetts Institute of Technology had a cathode-ray oscilloscope that displayed graphical solutions to differential equations. In 1952 the Whirlwind Group at M.I.T. built a computer that could display tactical air situations complete with points indicating aircraft and potential strategic targets. In 1953 the SAGE (Semi-Automatic Ground Environment) air traffic control system was being used by the United States military to convert radar information into crude (by today's standards), computer-generated pictures.[1]

There are other examples. Together they provide ample evidence that the beginnings of this technology can be traced back beyond 3 decades. The value in having computers draw pictures was recognized almost immediately. It did not take long for computer pioneers to begin exploring how electronic technology could be put to use generating pictorial information. What took longer was making the technology accessible and comprehensible to a wider spectrum of potential users. Even today much of the work being done with computer graphics is directed toward widening its application.

The Development of Interactivity

As computer graphics evolved and began to reach that wider audience, its accessibility came to be closely associated with the idea of interactivity. It is not difficult to see why. Interactivity is more than a valuable enhancement; without it, the operator's creativity may actually be impaired, the imagination stifled with rote tasks required by keeping track of the many standard operating procedures that maintain the system.

Yet interactivity is no simple thing. As the term is generally used, it describes a data processing context in which the system and the user work together to solve problems or to correlate and evaluate information. Usually the interactivity consists of the computer software prompting the user for information which is then processed in some predetermined way. The programing entailed in such software is complex. After the advent of graphics output devices, it took many more years of software development work for interactivity to begin to appear on graphics systems.

Nevertheless, the work had to be done. Consider what interactivity can do for the computer graphics system operator: while it may be interesting to see computer-generated graphics information displayed on a screen or output on a plotter, the display itself only becomes useful when the human operators are able to manipulate that display easily and quickly. Only then does the operator begin to see his or her own ideas take graphic form. Only then does computer graphics become a design tool rather than merely an output device. Interactivity empowers computer graphics as a practical and widely applicable extension of the user's imagination.

The Earliest Computer Graphics Systems

The groundwork for interactivity was begun in the late 1950s when "light guns" were becoming prevalent. The precursors of today's "light pen," they were used to designate points on the display screen which the computer could then recognize and store. The idea of interactivity was born. But it was still just an idea. It was not until 1962 that the real impetus behind interactivity began. At the Spring Joint Computer Conference in San Francisco Ivan Sutherland, a graduate of M.I.T., demonstrated his SKETCHPAD system which enabled on-line graphics compositions to be created for the first time.[2] This revolutionary new system set the stage for all subsequent developments in the area of interactive computer graphics.

Also at about this time, and also at M.I.T., Steve Coons began doing work in the development of surface patch creation, a type of geometry ideally suited to computer graphics modeling.[3] With Sutherland and Coons working together, it was not long before SKETCHPAD had been extended to produce images in three dimensions, and the rudiments of a formal graphics language began to evolve. Computer graphics began to develop more rapidly thereafter; computer-aided design was just around the corner.

The Beginning of Computer-Aided Design

At about the same time a similar program was underway at Itek Laboratories which would prove the value of computer graphics in real-world applications. Researchers there had begun the development of an on-line graphics system for use in the design of optic lenses. They wrote a program which directed a two-dimensional plotter to trace light ray paths and show how they would be deflected when traveling through variously shaped glass lenses. This system, called Digigraphics, was later acquired by Control Data Corporation and became the basis for their well-known Digigraphics computer graphics product line.[4]

A second important breakthrough came in 1964 with the demonstration at the Fall Joint Computer Conference in San Francisco of the DAC-1 (Design Augmented by Computer) system.[5] This system was developed at General Motors Research for use in the design of automobile and truck parts. For the first time, a system operator could sit at a graphics console and not only create but modify sketches on a display screen. These sketches could then be stored and used later in conjunction with numerically controlled machine tools to create actual automobile models.

The DAC-1 system was significant for several reasons—some of them technical, some of them philosophical. Computer graphics was now moving well beyond the relatively simple technology that enabled operators to construct and manipulate drawings. The new systems, as represented by DAC-1, were developing the ability to to act on the input data in wholesale, automatic ways such as those implied by scaling, mirroring, or rotation operations.

The computing systems were beginning to do more than just ask for and record input data; they could actually understand the geometry implied by the drawing and begin to manipulate it based on internal command-driven calculations. Systems no longer had to rely exclusively on calculations conducted by the user. A full-scale interactivity was developing between the system and the user. Graphics systems had begun to acquire what has come to be known as artificial intelligence—an awkward term that refers to the computer's ability to emulate human thought processes. The operator's mind was gradually being freed to concentrate on more purely creative tasks.

Making the Technology Useful

The implementation of more highly interactive systems required a whole new way of thinking about the possibilities of computer graphics. As systems developed more intelligence and versatility, users were becoming more efficient. The question was no longer, "Is this technology useful" but, "How can we make this technology *more* useful?" This new attitude led the way for computer graphics to evolve into computer-aided design, wherein the operator relies on the machine to do many of the routine calculations, thus freeing his or her own mind to work on the more creative aspects of design. Human creativity was rapidly becoming a more prominent component of the on-line decision making process.

This was an important breakthrough because it permitted the machine and the operator to concentrate on those tasks best suited to their abilities. Computers are very fast, very accurate, and have good memories, but they are not creative. Human operators, on the other hand, are slower, more prone to calculation errors and forgetfulness but can be highly creative and intuitive. Interactivity was the key to this symbiosis between operator and machine. The so-called "user interface" became paramount in the design of an effective computer graphics installation. It still is.

Computer graphics had by now developed far beyond the early technology in which a system had only output capabilities. Now graphics data could be input, manipulated, and output all on one system. Computer graphics systems had become creative tools capable of showing in visible form what the designer was thinking abstractly. This idea became singularly important as the technology grew and developed and full-scale CAD/CAM systems were born. Without a 2-way communication between operator and machine, computer-aided design and manufacturing is not possible.

Moreover, the communication must be very fast and comprehensive. These demands placed enormous pressure on system hardware manufacturers to build machines with spectacular processing, storage, and data transmission functions. Systems were required not only to maintain huge quantities of graphics information but the results of analytic routines evaluating that data as well. And it had to be done fast enough for the operator to feel his or her ideas were being translated into graphic form at a speed comparable to the rate at which the mind works.

Few system users could long tolerate a system that draws lines or figures many minutes or seconds after that line is drawn in his mind. It would be like drawing on paper with a pen and finding the ink to be invisible until after it had dried many minutes later. The demand is for systems that produce lines immediately after the command is entered, where the waiting time for data to be displayed on the screen is held to an absolute minimum.

Hardware Developments

Given this need for speed and for processing power, there has been enormous pressure to improve the hardware components of CAD/CAM systems. Current computer hardware developments have had an enormous impact on the improvement of modern CAD/CAM systems. In fact, hardware has to follow closely the advancements in software development. It is not much of an oversimplification to say that today's software becomes tomorrow's hardware. Hardware tools, after all, tend to be faster and more reliable than software tools. The better the hardware components of a graphics system, the better the system performance.

The first CAD/CAM systems were based on either IBM or Digital Equipment Corporation (DEC) central processing units. The DAC-1 console, for instance, announced in 1964, was first installed by IBM on its 7094 machine. The DEC PDP-9 machine arrived on the scene in 1966, making available for CAD/CAM applications both a storage tube and a stroke-vector cathode-ray tube. This machine and its successor, the PDP-15, established DEC's reputation for supplying support computers for engineering graphics workstations.[6] These machines became particularly well suited for CAD/CAM applications. But it was the third generation of the PDP family, represented by the PDP-11, that really helped found the CAD/CAM industry; this machine became a mainstay in CAD/CAM system hardware.

The importance of these hardware developments cannot be overstated. In the most general terms, it might even be said that CAD/CAM really came into its own with the development of 16-bit minicomputers and with the advent of the storage tube as standard display technology. Without these developments CAD/CAM might never have developed into the fully integrated systems we see today.

In the late 1960s and early 1970s, Applicon, Intergraph, and McAuto all introduced turnkey CAD/CAM systems on the DEC PDP-11. These systems were expensive ($1 million and more), but they were reliable and relatively fast for their time. Many of them, in fact, are still in use today.

Not long after this, several other 16-bit minicomputers came onto the market and began to spawn additional turnkey CAD/CAM systems. Among these was the Data General Nova which became the basis for Calma's CAD/CAM system, and the Sperry Univac V77 line of computers, used by Auto-trol Technology to support their design and drafting system.[7]

The next logical step in CPU (central processing unit) development was the advent of 32-bit architecture. By enlarging the size of the data path, compute-intensive applications such as CAD/CAM can be made to operate much faster and with a great deal more accuracy. In the mid-1970s DEC came out with its VAX line of 32-bit processors and Data General followed with a line of MV 32-bit machines. Both computers were picked up by turnkey CAD/CAM vendors as the basis for new and better systems.[8]

More recently there has been another development in computer hardware architecture: distributed processing. With the availability of high-speed microprocessor chips such as the Motorola 68000 and its successors, or the newly announced 32032 chip from National Semiconductor, more and more processing has been offloaded from the host computer to the workstation. The logical extension of this was the development of completely independent, stand-alone workstations that can share data. A number of such distributed systems are already being sold by CAD/CAM vendors to a variety of industries.

Other hardware developments have had their impact as well. For instance, the availability of high-resolution color display monitors has made them a standard component of CAD/CAM systems. The cheaper and faster raster tubes have begun to supplant the older storage tubes. Ergonomics has developed into nearly an artform.

In all of these developments the objectives have always been the same: to accommodate customers who have continually pressed for systems with better response time and with more accessibility. There will always be room for improvement. Nevertheless, clear standards have begun to develop which by now permeate the CAD/CAM industry.

Today's Industry Standards

Today interactivity is a standard in the CAD/CAM industry. We are at the point where the quality and versatility of the interactivity are being judged, not its existence. There are other standards. For instance, 32-bit hardware is nearly indispensible given the intense computing requirements of modern day CAD/CAM applications. No longer are 16-bit systems fast enough or accurate enough to support the mathematical requirements of today's analytical programs. As another example, color display monitors have become the norm, and they are components in more than 75% of the graphics workstation hardware now being sold. Designers and engineers have discovered what visual artists have always known: color is a powerful communications tool.

Coincident with the rise in the importance of color, raster display tubes have largely supplanted calligraphic tubes. Raster displays are faster and cheaper than vector displays and they have very nearly the same levels of resolution.[9]

Still another trend in CAD/CAM technology is the development of graphics workstations with more and more intelligence. Workstations that have the ability to offload work from the central processing unit enable the whole system to operate faster and more efficiently. Many experts believe that before too long the industry standard will move toward completely stand-alone workstations with networking capabilities that allow them all to share a common data base. A great many such systems are already being sold by major CAD/CAM manufacturers.

Finally, CAD/CAM applications are rapidly becoming more and more specialized, and the emphasis is moving toward enhanced design capabilities in addition to the established ability to do simple drafting. Increased specialization, in turn, implies a need for increased standardization in the way graphics data are formatted. Without it, specialized systems will be unable to share data. The industry is already responding to the need for workstation compatibility by developing standards such as the SIGGRAPH Graphical Kernel System (GKS) and the Initial Graphics Exchange Specification (IGES) being evaluated by the American National Standards Institute (ANSI).

At least one thing in all of this is very clear: computer graphics is a vital and rapidly moving industry, and in many market segments it has become an absolutely essential part of the design/ manufacturing cycle. The numbers bear this out. By the end of 1983, 28,501 CAD/CAM workstations had been installed worldwide, representing total industry revenues for the year of $2,175,000,000. By the end of 1984 the figures were 56,058 and $3,106,000,000 respectively; by the end of 1985 they will be 101,005 and $4,426,000,000.[10] By 1990, CAD/CAM may well be a $10 billion per year industry. These are staggering figures. They suggest the CAD/CAM revolution is just beginning.

Who's Who in CAD/CAM

In the last 10 to 15 years scores of companies have come and gone while trying to capitalize on the growing CAD/CAM market. It will doubtless take many more years before the industry settles down and competitive pressures weed out the strong companies from the weak. Nevertheless, a number of these turnkey CAD/ CAM system vendors have established themselves in various market segments and can be expected to be around, in some form, for the long-term.

IBM is now the largest CAD/CAM vendor, in terms of market share, despite having been in the business a relatively short time. In 1983 they owned nearly 21% of the total revenues, most of it coming from the mechanical side of the market. The largest vendor in terms of total installed workstations, however, is Computervision. They have nearly 10,000 workstations installed around the world and should maintain their position as number 2 in yearly CAD/CAM revenues. Two other companies should be mentioned in this first echelon of CAD/CAM vendors: Intergraph and Calma. Both have yearly revenues approaching one-quarter of a billion dollars. And, in the second echelon of CAD/CAM vendors, listed in order of size, are Applicon, McAuto, Auto-trol, Gerber, and Prime.[11]

Following the pack are dozens of other companies, some new, some old, who are struggling for their piece of the CAD/CAM pie. It is a highly competitive business, and when the customer knows what to look for, he or she can make that competition work to his advantage.

References

1. Carl Machover, *A Brief Personal History of Computer Graphics* (White Plains, NY: Machover Associates Corp.), p. 1.

2. I.E. Sutherland, "SKETCHPAD—A Man-Machine Graphical Communication System," in *Proceedings—Spring Joint Computer Conference, 1963* (Baltimore, MD: Spartan Books, Inc., 1963).

3. Machover, p.2.

4. M. David Prince, *Interactive Graphics for Computer-Aided Design* (Reading, MA: Addison-Wesley Publishing Co. 1969), p. 5.

5. Prince, p. 5.

6. Edward L. Busick, "CAD/CAM Workstation Trends," *Computer Graphics World* 7 (4) (April 1984): 59.

7. Busick, p. 59.

8. Busick, p. 59.

9. A more detailed discussion of raster and calligraphic display hardware can be found in Chapter 3. Additional discussion of the use of color with CAD/CAM can be found in Appendix I.

10. *CAD/CAM Industry Service Marketing Analysts' Sourcebook, Vol. 2, Appendix B* (San Jose, CA: Dataquest, 1983), p. 1.

11. *CAD/CAM Industry Service Marketing Analysts' Sourcebook, Vol. 2*, p. 11.

Additional Reading

Parslow, R.D. et. al. *Computer Graphics: Techniques and Applications.* New York: Plenum Press, 1969. See especially "Part 1."

Chapter 2
The Viability of CAD/CAM Technology Today: Where It Is and What It Can Do

Computers are everywhere. They bill us for water and electricity, they send us tax statements, dun us for mortgage payments, handle our bank accounts, coordinate our phone calls, and make our travel reservations; they control many of our most personal transactions and communications. Computers are in our offices, our homes, our cars, our appliances. They are a fact of our lives—yet many people are still wary.

They have reason to be. Computers have required us to make enormous adjustments in the way we conduct many of our day-to-day activities. The same is true of CAM systems—and more. CAD/CAM influences the way we run our businesses.

Consider just the most obvious effects a CAD/CAM system can have on a business. By making the product design cycle of a company faster, more efficient, and more accurate, CAD/CAM will influence nearly every department within that corporate structure. As a result, management must be prepared to act much more rapidly than ever before on product development decisions. Production workers must be prepared to receive product specifications faster, more often, and in greater detail. Marketing personnel must be prepared to provide faster support for new products and faster analysis of market trends. Sales representatives must become conversant about more products and be more flexible in finding potential customers. The research and development staff must be prepared to react more quickly to new design ideas and new design tools. Engineers and drafters must accommodate a whole new set of tools and information. All of these consequences entail a whole new way of thinking, managing, and conducting daily business. People have every reason to remain wary of this new technology.

If we can understand the potential benefits of CAD/CAM, we will adjust better. We will likely be more accepting of this new technology and more willing to put up with the havoc it will play on the existing procedures we use to conduct business.

It is best to start from the beginning and find out exactly what computer graphics technology can do and how it can be made useful in design and manufacturing environments. Some of the answers to these 2 questions are surprising!

A Tool for the Mind

Perhaps the simplest way to regard CAD/CAM is as a tool for the mind rather than a tool just for the hands. It extends our mental abilities, makes the creative part of design work faster and more visual, allows us, in fact, to see what we are thinking. To this extent it may even enable us to extend our imaginations into areas never ventured before. This is not overstatement. But make no mistake—CAD/CAM is, after all, a tool, and only as good as the people who use it.

Computer graphics, as we have already seen, allows us to draw with a computer rather than a pencil. But CAD/CAM allows us to do more. It allows us to draw and then to evaluate what we have created. This is a very important extension to simple graphics, because it is in the evaluation that the creative talents of the engineer and drafter can be most revealed.

Yet while an integrated CAD/CAM system may be new and unusual, the tasks required of it are much the same as those required of engineering and drafting tools in use half a century ago. CAD/CAM requires no new engineering or design concepts. Design analysis, mathematical and mechanical modeling, drafting, documentation, process planning, machine tooling, fabrication, and group technology are all old concepts and were around long before CAD/CAM became established in the marketplace.

The Design Cycle

For the drafter and the engineer, the design process remains largely the same whether a CAD/CAM system is installed or not.

The ideas are the same, and it is important to recognize that the process is more intellectual than mechanical.

The design cycle begins when a design need is perceived within a company and a specific goal is set to satisfy that need. With that much established, the drafters and engineers can set to work.

Their first task is to analyze the problem and to break it down into its constituent parts. This might well be a very long and involved first step. If the need is for the design of a more fuel efficient automobile, for instance, a host of factors must be considered. What seating capacity? What price range? To what extent can looks be compromised for aerodynamics? What kind and size of engine is best? Do we design a new engine? Will the body be metal or fiberglass?

On the other hand, if the need is for a slotted, hexagonal head machine screw, the analysis is much simpler—but a number of factors must still be considered. What stresses will it be required to withstand? How long should it be? What is the thread size? The diameter? The head size? Nevertheless, the process of analysis is much the same no matter the magnitude of the task. The CAD/CAM system may help, but it cannot replace the knowledge and expertise of the experienced engineer. No qualified engineer or designer was ever made obsolete because of CAD/CAM.

With the problem analyzed and sorted out into individual tasks, the more strictly creative work begins. The designer must come up with an idea that will effectively satisfy the established needs. Here again, this is work that no computer can do without explicit direction. Creativity is province of the designer alone.

Next comes the analysis of the design proposal. This determines whether the design is adequate. The proposal is subjected to minute mathematical analysis as well as aesthetic and qualitative judgments. Based on this analysis, refinements may be suggested or required and the proposal respecified. The cycle then begins again. The proposal is sharpened and improved, it is subjected to careful scrutiny, and new changes may be warranted. With the last iteration, the drawings, specifications, and fabrication information are produced, and the design is finally sent off to manufacturing. The manufacturing department may then have its own suggestions on how to make the product better, simpler, or cheaper to create. This information is also passed back into the design cycle and the refinements continue.

The entire process is characterized by repetition and analysis. The process does not change. But it does lend itself perfectly to computerization. A computer excels in those situations where iteration and integration make up a large part of the task.

The Power of Integration

The real power of CAD/CAM as a design tool, however, is larger than simply speeding up the design cycle. CAD/CAM also has a built-in ability to integrate all the tasks related to the entire design and manufacturing process. By coordinating both the tasks and the data generated by those tasks, the CAD/CAM system is a ready-made focal point for the entire design and manufacturing operation.

By breaking down these tasks even further we can see how this integration might work. Consider the individual tasks that go into taking a product from idea through production. Take as an example, designing a glass mold.

The company is in need of a mold design which can be used to manufacture a wine glass. Using the specifications required by the product design, the mold designer first creates a mathematical model of the mold and of the finished wine glass. By doing this, the designer can account for all the important design considerations of the mold at once and then analyze the possibilities on-line. With the entire product depicted in purely mathematical terms, the designer can consider fluid flow, stresses, the implications of applying heat and cold, densities, as well as the more visual properties of complex curves and surfaces, 3-dimensional space, and intersections. The CAD/CAM system totally eliminates the need to build a physical model of either the wine glass or the mold.

When the mold designer is satisfied with the mathematical model, he can proceed to build a mechanical model of the wine glass mold. The mechanical model represents a practical application of the information generated by the mathematical model. It takes into account such real world considerations as commercially available materials, standard manufacturing tools, and their tolerences. Moreover, the part image (in this case, the finished glass) and the mold image can be displayed on the workstation screen simultaneously so the designer can compare the 2 visually.

Next, the designer translates all this information into standard engineering drawings. The drawings are a record of all the physical attributes of the design and might well depict the mold from a variety of angles. The system will help create these varied perspectives automatically.

There is a danger in all of this, however. The object in automating the design process with CAD/CAM is to create engineering drawings that are useful but not redundant. By speeding up the ability of the designer to create drawings, the CAD/CAM system may encourage a proliferation of unnecessary drawings. However, if these drawings are grouped together in families according to the type of part depicted or according to the perspective depicted, the system can actually reduce the number of new designs being created.

The efficacy of the system lies subtantially in how it is managed. Through proper management, designers will be able to find existing drawings that will fit the needs of their current project. In this way, design retrieval functions are streamlined and costs are further reduced.

Design Documentation

The next step after creation of appropriate drawings, is design documentation. Here again, it can all be done on-line using existing information derived from the modeling and drawing steps. The wine glass mold must be described for purposes of bills of material, for adherence to design and drafting standards, for quality assurance checks, for tooling data, for billing, and for all other specifications the company may want to keep track of.

The CAD/CAM system can make this task go faster, can store the information easier, and can associate related documentation more efficiently than can be done off-line. Furthermore, it actually decreases the amount of redundant documentation the designer needs to keep track of by automatically creating the necessary information during the modeling and drawing procedures.

The design work, by the time the documentation is completed, is largely finished. Production is now asked to fabricate the part based on the information provided by the designer.

Good communication between the engineering and production departments is crucial to making the physical part. The transfer of information from one department to the other must be clear and thorough. And with all the information already auto- mated and on-line, the manufacturing department has a perfect library of information right at its fingertips. It is, in fact, the very same information used by the designer to create his model. These data are both complete and up-to-date; obsolete or corrected data simply do not exist since the system continually and universally updates the information as it is being developed.

With a single up-to-date data base to draw from, the commu- nications problems of old become moot. When the CAD/CAM installation is properly implemented, the design and man- ufacturing requirements exist together in a single data base. The manufacturing department is free to use the information to create tapes for its numerically controlled machine tools or for its man- ufacturing robots. In this way, the design data are applied to the manufacturing tasks directly. The result is faster manufacturing turnaround and much less room for error.

Group Technology

The last piece of the puzzle is group technology. Group tech- nology refers to a manufacturing philosophy which recognizes the advantages of associating similar discrete manufactured parts. These groups of similar parts can be manufactured more effi- ciently if done together through mass production techniques. Group technology is the final step in total system integration, and it also can be handled by the CAD/CAM system using only one consistent and current data base.

To summarize, CAD/CAM provides a ready-made method of integrating the following production steps:

1. Design Creation
2. Design Analysis
3. Mathematical Modeling
4. Mechanical Modeling
5. Creation of Engineering Drawings
6. Drawing Cataloging and Retrieval
7. Documentation (including bills of material, technical illustration, invoicing)

8. Production Planning
9. Machine Tooling/Robotics
10. Group Technology

By properly using a CAD/CAM system a company's entire design and manufacturing cycle can be made to work efficently using a single, continually updated data base. The benefits are both numerous and obvious. For one, redundancy of data and of work is kept to a minimum. For another, the data are always current. Also it is easier to retrieve data; documentation is updated automatically; and associated data are stored together. In addition, new data, such as required by new perspectives or analyses, can be generated automatically using the graphics data that already exist on-line.

What Are the Drawbacks?

The drawbacks to CAD/CAM may not be so obvious, but they can be devastating to even the best plans. The most debilitating of these comes from the leap entailed in moving directly from manual drafting and record keeping to CAD/CAM. It is like putting a jet engine in a Volkswagon. The car may go fast for a little while, but the whole thing will shake apart if the chassis is not reinforced sufficiently to handle the stress.

In other words, CAD/CAM will highlight the inadequacies of the weakest areas of work. This can be brutal to the people and to the disciplines that cannot keep up. As one writer puts it: "If drawings and bills of material, and part number systems within a company are being used poorly now, a CAD/CAM system will exacerbate the problem."[1]

When such unsatisfactory results occur, the finger is often pointed at the CAD/CAM system—hardly a fair accusation, but it is usually more comfortable than pointing at people or organizations. Any computer will only be as valuable as the data put into it. It is the cardinal rule of data processing: garbage in, garbage out. If a company is utilizing an inadequate inventory control system, that system will not improve just because it is automated. The automation, in fact, will make the inadequacies much more glaring, and the result may be complete chaos. Therefore it is extremely important when implementing CAD/CAM not just to evaluate the needs for this technology, but to evaluate the existing disciplines it is expected to enhance.

If management is unwilling to evaluate the existing operating conditions, standards, and procedures, the implementation of CAD/CAM is very likely to fail—for a number of compounding reasons. For one, management policies will be unorganized because the CAD/CAM system will be isolated from standard operating procedures. This will likely produce a growing feeling among low-level managers that the system can never be made useful to them. For another, no interdepartmental communications paths will have been established. This could result in the feeling there is no long-term commitment to CAD/CAM. For still another, operators (the people actually using the system), will have had no input in the way the system was implemented. This leads to lack of drawing standards, poor system management, and alienation of system users. Such circumstances are really unforgiveable, especially since the opportunity to evaluate standard operating conditions will almost certainly suggest improvements in those procedures even if the CAD/CAM system is never implemented.

What Does This Mean for the Employee?

The trick then is being prepared for the implementation before it ever begins. That preparation must include everyone. After all, everyone involved in the project will be forced to change the way they think about their jobs. They are being asked to accept a new and complex tool, and they should be prepared to confront considerable changes.

The worst way to implement CAD/CAM is by setting short-term goals. That will ensure failure. A better way to implement CAD/CAM is gradually and based on long-term goals. In other words, planning the implementation of CAD/CAM is more important than the implementation itself; more important than the installation, or the management, or the maintenance, or even the evaluation of the equipment. Planning must be done in a big way—and it must involve everyone.

Early CAD/CAM systems required very specialized, highly trained personnel. Very often that meant hiring a systems analyst, a software specialist, and a hardware engineer. Even the system operators had to be technically trained computer specialists. The most basic elements of the technology were changing so rapidly and system integration was so rudimentary that the personnel had to be very knowledgeable in order to meet the challenges. An early book on CAD/CAM, published in 1966, contains these words: "... it is very important, *at this time* italics theirs, that the prospective computer graphics user allow for the inclusion of skilled computer technologists on his computer-aided design staff—the number, of course, varying with the ambitiousness of the project. This requirement, however, will diminish rapidly in the coming years as equipment becomes more stabilized."[2]

This prediction came true. CAD/CAM systems are more accessible and standardized than they have ever been. This does not, however, alleviate the responsibility of the operators to entertain new ideas and accept new methodologies. It simply means that computer expertise is no longer a prerequisite for CAD/CAM operators.

It is more important that the CAD/CAM operators understand the system's applications than its mechanisms. It is much easier to teach an engineer how to use the system than it is to teach a CAD/CAM system analyst how to be an engineer. A drafter can pick up the fundamentals of CAD/CAM system operations in a matter of weeks, but his or her drafting abilities are the product of many years of study and practice. Given this, applying the tool is much more important than understanding its many minute parts. And while a CAD/CAM system is an enormously complicated thing to put together, it is designed precisely to be as easy as possible to use. If a novice computer operator cannot learn it easily, the value of the system is greatly diminished. Above all, a CAD/CAM system should be accessible.

How Far Can CAD/CAM Take Us?

We should keep this issue of accessibility in mind when we come to evaluate the overall viability of a CAD/CAM system. We should also be realistic in our expectations. No one can learn to use a CAD/CAM system overnight. Just because some simple operations are automated and just because we learn them, doesn't mean we have mastered the system. Increases in productivity lie far beyond simply drawing geometric figures faster.

It is very hard, therefore, to quantify exactly how far these increases in productivity go. That makes it difficult to translate the savings into dollars for the purpose of putting together a business plan. It is unfortunate, but many businesses that could benefit from an installed CAD/CAM system never have the opportunity to because department managers cannot figure out how to justify the expenditure to upper management.

It is no wonder. Many of the benefits of CAD/CAM remain well hidden. Consider how the system operator learns to use this new tool. First, there is the matter of simply learning how to operate the keyboard, digitizer, bitpad, and other system components. Second, is the matter of being familiar with the software, determining what it can and cannot do. With that much mastered it is easy to determine how much faster it is to produce a standard engineering drawing. The difficulty is in making management realize that this is only the tip of the iceberg. Faster drawing creation represents the beginning of productivity increases, not the end.

Increasing Drafting Productivity

CAD/CAM systems can entail a whole new set of drafting philosophies, all of which enhance productivity. For instance, most systems now on the market have a number of built-in functions that make new and useful drafting techniques automatic. Layering, for example, enables drafters to create drawings in logical segments that can be stored separately for easy identification; but the segments can still be output together, in one single piece, which illustrates the entire drawing at once. The method is analogous to the anatomical drawings we are used to seeing in biology texts. The skeleton, nerves, internal organs, blood vessels, and muscles are all represented on individual overlays of clear plastic. They can be viewed individually, or, by laying them on top of one another, all together, to show how the pieces fit in relation to one another. Layering with a graphics system uses the same principle except the overlays are logical rather than physical. The uses for this are myriad. Layers can be used to separate English and metric dimensioning information, inventory data, textual information, electrical requirements, plumbing, machine tool paths, and a host of other things. The result is cleaner, less cluttered drawings.

Another example of a productivity enhancement for drafting might involve automating auxiliary views of a design. By pressing the right button or by entering the right command, a drawing could be turned 90 degrees in one direction or another. Three-dimensional designs could be rotated on any axis or displayed in any of several projections. Perhaps it would be useful to zoom in on a detailed portion of a drawing, or to move back from the drawing to put the entire representation in proper perspective. All of these functions can be automated with CAD/CAM thus enabling, say, the manufacturing department to see all aspects of a design and thereby better understand it, resulting in much faster product fabrication.

The potential is really endless. Productivity increases are limited only when system management philosophies are limited. As an additional example, consider a drafting center for an architectural firm that specializes in designing warehouses. Much of the design work is repetitive and can be carried over from one job to the next. In such a situation, standard components of each drawing can be automated by creating macros. These macros are nothing more than a series of graphics system commands strung together and executed as a single unit to build, for example, a standard floor plan or a standard staircase, or a standard door and door frame. The system can do the work in seconds and the drafter is relieved from recreating that part of the design each time it must be inserted into a drawing.

Other macro programs could be useful. A set of commands might be put together that change the dimensioning of a drawing automatically from English to metric units—or that automatically scale an entire drawing and rotate it to a desired orientation—or that generate a bill of materials list for complicated engineering drawings.

To take it one step further, remember that entire designs can be stored on the system. When the drafter receives a job that has specifications similar to a stored drawing, he merely retrieves it, brings it into working storage, and edits those portions of the design that are not consistent with the specifications of the new job. Productivity increases are thus compounded. The original job is speeded up, and that job, in turn, is used to speed up the next job even further. This illustrates the need to maintain a complete and up-to-date data base that can be accessed easily by all users.

Data base management becomes a singularly important aspect of overall CAD/CAM system management.

Improving Design Analysis

Design analysis is another important task that can be handled automatically by a properly integrated CAD/CAM system. This is particularly important in an application like piping plant design where drawings are often complex and must adhere to precise industry specifications. A CAD/CAM system with piping design applications software can give the user automatic feedback on such characteristics as fluid capacities, material chemistry, stress limitations, and coupling requirements. It can also generate orthographic plans, elevation data, equipment parts lists, cost estimates, flow diagrams, process and instrumentation diagrams, and bills of materials. The system can even access and control complex engineering analysis programs and provide instant feedback on the viability of various design alternatives.

These tools are available. It is up to industry to apply them and make them useful. Business is well advised to keep an open mind toward this technology and not focus too narrowly on any one aspect of CAD/CAM. Current technology can do a lot more than just speed up creation of production drawings.

Increasing Engineering Productivity

Virtually all engineering tasks can also be automated. Modeling, for instance, can be a very useful and powerful tool for conducting product simulations and design analyses. One method of modeling is by simply manipulating existing graphics primitives. Primitives are the most basic entities of the graphics system and include such constructions as cones, rectangles, spheres, triangles, and other 2- and 3-dimensional objects. These constructions can be manipulated by the system automatically using features such as shading, scaling, rotating, cross-sectioning, and merging, to emulate virtually any design idea.

A more sophisticated approach to modeling is with specialized CAD/CAM software that actually builds solid models on the system. These solids modeling applications employ complex geometric functions to define the boundaries of models, and, by extension, their volumetric, surface, and edge characteristics. The result is a complete solid object, consisting entirely of mathematical representations, that can be studied as though it were an actual manufactured object. The solidity derives from the fact that any point on or within the object can be defined mathematically.

The uses for this kind of technology are manifold. Not only does it allow engineers to view product models and to simulate their physical characteristics, but it provides realistic pictures of these constructions that can be used in creating exploded views, parts manuals, and manufacturing drawings. In addition, solids modeling permits computation of all the physical factors that may be important to the production of each part, such as weight, density, center of gravity, volume, and sensitivity to heat and stress. Even tool cutter paths can be calculated and translated directly into numerical control tapes.

Finite Element Analysis

But perhaps most important to overall engineering objectives, solid models can be used to conduct sophisticated finite element analysis. By this process, individual parts are reduced to discrete physical elements which can be analyzed independently with regard to required stresses or displacements. In this way, small portions of each part can be analyzed based on the loads and stresses they will be subject to when the part is manufactured and put to use. Part failures are thus kept to a minimum.

This kind of meticulous and thorough analysis is made much easier through use of the CAD/CAM system. Automating these functions makes them go faster, reduces the errors so common to manual evaluations, and eliminates the tendency for engineers to look for shortcuts in their analysis regimen. Also keep in mind that the engineering analysis is based on the identical set of data that were originally created during the design and drafting portions of the design/manufacturing cycle. Such tight integration, by itself, removes much of the danger of error that comes from using incorrect or outdated information. In short, the better the design analysis becomes, the closer the manufacturing plant can come to optimization of parts, personnel, and costs.

Other Analytical Benefits

CAD/CAM can influence a company's engineering systems in many other ways as well. It can streamline all physical processes, and permit reevaluation of current engineering methods and reporting procedures. CAD/CAM improves and expedites quality assurance techniques, and it lends itself naturally to maintaining accurate and complete documentation and to keeping accurate records of part numbers and bills of materials.

The proper installation of a fully integrated CAD/CAM system forces a company to evaluate all design and production methods and to begin appropriate standardization of those methods. Usually this evaluation proves profitable; but it can be traumatic for those who are unprepared. Management would be wise to keep both these things in mind. The application of CAD/CAM is always a complicated business.

The Application of CAD/CAM

CAD/CAM technology has come a long way since SKETCH-PAD. It is already being applied to a wide variety of different industries. It is used for everything from air traffic control to weapons research, from cartography to sports medicine, from circuit analysis to structural steel analysis. CAD/CAM is being applied to all aspects of drafting and manufacturing, from drawing sketches for movie sets to directing enormous robots that assemble battleships. Its versatility is still being explored.

The first applications of CAD/CAM were mostly in electronics. This was because CAD/CAM was not an accepted technology beyond the confines of the computer industry itself. Slowly people began to realize the need for CAD/CAM in such markets as aeronautics, civil engineering, and architecture. The newer, more complicated designs were stretching manual drafting techniques beyond the breaking point. CAD/CAM was the inevitable answer. By now the technology has a strong technological and financial base on which to work. Potential CAD/CAM users can afford to be picky about the systems they finally purchase. There is no more excuse for buying a second-rate or inappropriate system.

The CAD/CAM Marketplace Today

Today there are 4 different kinds of CAD/CAM vendors in the marketplace. First are the subsidiary companies that sell CAD/CAM technology from within a department or division of a larger corporation. The CAD/CAM division of IBM is an example, as is McAuto, owned by McDonnell-Douglas; Calma, owned by General Electric; and Applicon, owned by Schlumberger. Most of these CAD/CAM subsidiaries do a great deal of business with their parent companies, selling not only turnkey systems but acting as service bureaus. These companies are at their best when handling large accounts and providing service because they have such large resources from which to draw on. But they are also burdened with complex bureaucracies, which makes it difficult for them to react quickly to market trends or to incorporate into their product lines new technology developed outside their own research and development departments.

Second are the established turnkey vendors. These companies offer a variety of CAD/CAM systems in various price ranges for several different industries. These companies have been in CAD/CAM for 10 years or more and have established reputations in the development of new technology. Among the companies in this category are Computervision, Intergraph, and Auto-trol Technology. These companies, because of their relatively smaller size, sometimes have trouble providing good service, but they react well to their customer's technology needs and can offer reliable, usable systems to a variety of industry segments.

Third are the new, entrepreneurial CAD/CAM vendors. These companies tend to be small, young, and very innovative. Their combined market share is only about 5%, but each company excels in providing a single, high-quality system to a narrow market segment. Very often, entrepreneurial companies market mini- or microsystems that are useful to customers with small and specialized CAD/CAM needs. Such customers are, in fact, well advised to purchase equipment from entrepreneurial CAD/CAM vendors.

Fourth are the service bureaus. These companies specialize in doing CAD/CAM work for other firms who have minimal or inconsistent needs. Service bureaus are becoming more and more prevalent and are often the best solution for companies who cannot afford their own CAD/CAM facilities or who are not yet ready to commit to such facilities. Service bureaus not only do CAD/CAM-related tasks, but they can conduct training classes and seminars for companies who may be contemplating the purchase of their own equipment in the future.

Doing business with each of these vendor types has both benefits and drawbacks. Large companies are difficult to bargain with and slow to move their products toward the latest technology developments, but they generally provide good service and reliable products. Established turnkey vendors are more flexible to individual customer requirements and have shorter upgrade cycles, but they are susceptible to economic downturns and have difficulty servicing existing systems. The entrepreneurs sometimes have the best, state-of-the-art solutions for one or 2 narrow applications, but they often have very little management or marketing stability and can be risky investments. Service bureaus are good for small accounts, but cannot sustain a company with complicated CAD/CAM needs. It is up to each user to determine what kind of vendor is best, and it is important that potential customers understand what sort of a CAD/CAM vendor they are dealing with before they sign a sales contract. Dealing with the wrong kind of company, just as dealing with the wrong kind of system, can create long-term problems for the user.

It is also up to each vendor to determine which customers are best. The big and established vendors, for instance, tend to pursue accounts with Fortune 500 companies. While the competition may be fierce, they believe it is to their benefit to sell large accounts which function to centralize these vendors' service requirements, reduce average installation costs, and generate greater potential for system upgrades. Other vendors, usually the smaller, entrepreneurial type companies, would rather sell to a specific industry or industry group. This allows them to concentrate their research and development efforts on what they do best and know most about.

What to Look out for

Most companies buying CAD/CAM systems today have never bought this technology before. They are what marketing people call "immature" customers. Such a business environment encourages the proliferation of exaggerated claims or of genuinely inadequate products. It is unfortunate, but customers must be on the lookout for CAD/CAM sales representatives making ridiculous claims about the systems they represent. No CAD/CAM system can be all things to all people.

As with other products, a clue to overselling is superlatives. Be wary of any system touted to be the best, the newest, the fastest, the lowest-priced, or the most dependable because it is likely to be none of those things. CAD/CAM technology is much too complex for simple-minded generalizations. Look instead for a system that is described by terms that are comprehensible and consistent with the vocabulary of the industry in which it is being sold. Listen for specifics that mean something to users. "High resolution" is vague at best, but "1024 X 1024 pixels" is something with real, quantifiable substance.

Another thing to be wary of is the low-cost CAD/CAM system. As with any purchase, the customer usually gets what he pays for, and a $5,000 CAD/CAM system will have very limited functionality.

CAD/CAM systems are, nevertheless, coming down in price. What used to cost half a million dollars can now be purchased for about one hundred thousand. The trend toward reduced costs will continue, but with a caveat. Most "mature" CAD/CAM customers looking for bargains are not willing to sacrifice functionality for savings. They want a system that displays in color, can do modeling and analysis, and is fast. They want to pay as little as possible for it, but they are not willing to give up any of the tools they have come to expect from CAD/CAM. This limits how far price reductions can go. Even as hardware costs are coming down every year, software development costs are going up. It seems unlikely that a $5,000 CAD/CAM system will do full-time engineers or drafters much good in the forseeable future. Customers who insist on starting with low-cost systems, however, are advised to use them solely to learn about CAD/CAM and its applications. After users have been acclimated to this technology on a low-cost system, they would be better off throwing it away and purchasing a full-function system with which to do real production work rather than trying to upgrade a clearly inadequate system. The results will be much more satisfying.

References

1. Charles S. Knox, *CAD/CAM Systems Planning and Implementation* (New York: Marcel Dekker, Inc., 1983), p. 12.

2. R.A. Siders et al., *Computer Graphics: A Revolution in Design* (Cambridge, MA: American Management Association Inc.), p. 118-19.

Additional Reading

Angell, I.O. *A Practical Introduction to Computer Graphics.* New York: Halsted Press, 1981.

Bylinsky, G. "A New Revolution is on the Way." *Fortune* (October 5, 1981): 106-14.

Greenberg, Donald, et al. *The Computer Image: Applications of Computer Graphics.* Reading, MA: Addison-Wesley Publishing Co., 1982.

Scott, Joan, ed. *Computergraphia: New Visions of Form, Fantasy, and Function.* London: Gulf Publishing Co., 1984.

Chapter 3
Standard System Components

Computer-aided design/computer-aided manufacturing systems are available in great variety. Many are unique. It is not uncommon for a system to be tailored specifically to the needs of an individual company or even an individual user. Despite the difficulty of supporting such systems, most vendors, even large, established companies, are willing to customize their CAD/CAM equipment.

Every user's requirements are a little different. Some customers may need 3 or 4 plotters, others may need none; some use digitizers heavily, others do not; some want independent engineering workstations, others operate more efficiently with a centralized system under the control of a single manager; some require huge amounts of on-line disk space, while others use relatively little; some want mechanical software applications, others want architectural. The variations are endless.

CAD/CAM technology has evolved to the point where the requirements of a diverse community of users can be accommodated. And through standardized hardware and software interfaces, system configurations are easier to change than ever before. Therefore, a "typical" turnkey CAD/CAM system is an idea of the past; nevertheless, there are typical CAD/CAM system components. For instance, it is hard to imagine an efficient CAD/CAM system without a well-designed workstation. Most systems also have a hard copy unit, and some kind of on-line data storage device, or perhaps additional input devices, or specialized display hardware. Customers should be aware of these possibilities so they do not end up with system components they do not need or without components they could use. Very little is really typical in CAD/CAM anymore, but there is room for some generalizing on the subject of system components.

Graphics Workstations

Central to a good CAD/CAM system, perhaps even more important than central processing unit (CPU) hardware, is the graphics workstation. The workstation is where the operator conducts the vast majority of his or her work. In many ways, the graphics workstation is the user's working environment. It is desk, communications tool, filing cabinet, and diversion. The operator's concentration is likely to be directed on or around the workstation throughout most of the working day.

Graphics workstations have many forms, each based on a different idea of what a working environment should be. They are host-dependent and stand-alone, corresponding to a centralized or decentralized management structure; portable and immovable, to fit various office and factory environments; expensive and inexpensive, based on budget and functional requirements; attractive and unsightly, in concert with taste; modular and packaged, depending on the adaptability of working space; color and black and white, to suit visualization demands. It is best to talk about them in terms of their function rather than their manifold physical variations.

First and foremost, the graphics workstation is the point of interactivity between the user and the CAD/CAM system. It accepts the operator's input and reacts in predictable ways while responding to that input. It is important, therefore, that the workstation be easy and comfortable to use and that both input and output is direct and comprehensible.

Workstations generally contain a number of functional parts. The most important part is the monitor or cathode-ray tube, on which the graphics data are represented in pictorial form. The display is driven by a display buffer and controller. The display buffer stores the display list, which is the sequence of bytes that defines the graphics information being painted on the screen. The controller retrieves the information from the display buffer and, in conjunction with other information derived from the central processor, paints the screen with the appropriate graphics data.

Input to the system derives from a lightpen, joystick, mouse, keyboard, tablet, or similar device that operates back through the controller. Often the workstation has some other local intelligence capabilities such as memory or an independent processor. All of this hardware is housed in specially designed cabinetry which includes some kind of working surface or working area. Together, these elements make up the graphics workstation or graphics console.

Three types of graphics display hardware are used most often: vector displays (sometimes called "calligraphic"), raster displays, and plasma/flat panel displays. There are benefits and drawbacks to each.

Vector Display Hardware

The distinguishing characteristic of vector display devices is that they display lines by drawing them directly on the screen from one end point to the other. The positions of the end points are defined according to a coordinate system and the line is written by an electron beam focused on a phosphor screen. The line becomes visible from the phosphorescent glow emitted by the screen. An electrostatic or magnetic field directs the electron beam to the specified coordinates.

The phosphorescent glow that makes each line visible persists only a short time. Therefore, each line must be redrawn at regular intervals if the display image is to remain visible. This redrawing, called "refreshing," must be conducted fast enough to give the illusion that the image is drawn permanently. The advantage of vector displays is their accuracy; but their expense relative to raster displays has led to an increasing preference for the latter.

An early and very popular version of the vector display hardware is the direct view storage tube (DVST). This type of display features the standard vector display technology described above—with one important addition. A storage grid is placed between the display screen and the electron beam. This grid stores the graphics data as a positive charge which is then transferred to the phosphorescent screen by a flood of electrons passing through the grid. These direct view storage tubes are able to maintain the displayed image for long periods without being refreshed. They have also proven to be very dependable and relatively inexpensive to produce. The disadvantage is that they are slow and have no mechanism for erasing portions of the displayed image. To alter an image, the entire screen must be redrawn. This makes them difficult to tolerate in settings requiring a high degree of interactivity.

Raster Display Hardware

Raster display devices operate more like a television equipped with a high-speed computer memory. This memory (usually called the "frame buffer") stores the image data in digital form. The data are then read through a digital-to-analog converter and displayed as video output on the screen.

If the display is set up to generate color output, it is equipped with 3 electron guns, each corresponding to a different primary color. The colors most often used are red, green, and blue. These colors are mixed on the screen in different proportions to make all the possible hues. The electron beams are directed onto the phosphor screen with a focusing magnet and various deflection coils and acceleration grids.

On a raster display screen the phosphor is distributed evenly across the surface in a pattern of tiny dots arranged in horizontal lines. Each dot can be made to glow red, green, or blue depending on which electron gun is trained on it. Each color patch is too minute for the human eye to pick out individually; therefore, the colors blend together to make the displayed image appear more naturalistic. The principle is the same as that employed a century ago by the pointillist painters.

The displayed image is actually defined as a series of coordinate positions stored in digital memory. Each position, called a picture element or "pixel," is given an X and Y location and assigned an intensity or color value. On the screen, each pixel corresponds to about 8 phosphor dots. The image is then built, pixel by pixel, according to data stored in the frame buffer. The resolution of the image is a function of the number of pixels represented horizontally and vertically on the screen. Modern raster display screens are frequently using 1024 X 1024 pixels of resolution, thus requiring well over a million individual memory locations to contain the data painted on the screen.

After the graphics data are stored in the frame buffer memory, they are drawn on the screen in much the same way as a television image is drawn. The electron beams move horizontally from left to right along each row of pixel locations, gradually moving from the top of the screen to the bottom. Most raster displays are interlaced, meaning that the beam skips every other line each trip down the face of the tube. The first complete scan illuminates the even numbered lines of pixels, while the next illuminates the odd numbered lines. In this way, the image is created so rapidly the eye detects no distracting flicker from the screen. Each complete pass on either the odd or the even lines is called a "frame," and the information reflecting one complete frame is held in the frame buffer at one time.

Among the advantages raster displays have over vector displays is their ability to do effective shading and to emulate solid objects in black and white or in color. One of the drawbacks to raster display is the large amount of memory they require in the frame buffer, which makes them somewhat less reliable than vector displays. The large memory also requires very high data transmission rates for them to be effective, and that can create additional problems. More generally, however, the versatility of raster has made this technology very common in modern graphics workstations, and the industry trend today is to use raster in favor of vector technology.

Plasma Display and Other Flat Panel Hardware

Plasma display technology is not widely used in the graphics industry despite having been available for many years. Part of the reason is that, until recently, plasma display screens have been too small to be useful in drafting and engineering applications. Nonetheless, there are some advantages to this kind of display technology, and a good deal of development work is being done in this area.

Traditional plasma display devices consist of 2 facing plates of glass between which is captured a layer of neon gas. The interior surfaces of the glass are coated with a conductor and contain rows and columns of intersecting electrodes. When sufficient low voltage electricity is applied through the electrodes the gas ionizes and glows orange. The image produced is a matrix of discrete dots corresponding to the intersections of the electrode strips. Only at the intersection of electrodes which have both been energized is there sufficent voltage to ionize the gas.

The advantage of plasma displays is that they can be contained in a single flat cabinet making them very convenient for desk tops or other places where space is minimal. They also require, relative to cathode-ray tubes, much lower operating voltages. Among the disadvantages are low resolution and high cost. Nevertheless, they are very dependable and offer a display with good brightness and contrast.

Several other types of flat panel technology are available and deserve mention. One of the more interesting examples is the flat panel cathode-ray tube display now being offered by Sony Corporation. They have developed a television using a small, flat CRT screen in which the electron beam runs parallel to the face of the screen and is then bent 90 degrees toward the phosphor on the screen by a special deflector mechanism. The result is a very compact, black and white display device. Its applicability to computer graphics remains in doubt only because the screen is so small (2 inches by 2 inches).

Another flat panel display device is based on electroluminescence technology. These devices operate much like plasma displays except that they use luminescent solids, such as zinc sulfide, instead of neon gas. Light is emitted by the luminescent material when sufficent voltage is transmitted through the grid of electrodes embedded between the sheets of glass. Here again, the display screens are as yet quite small, but the image quality is good.

Liquid crystal display also has some applicability to graphics systems. The liquid crystal material, usually indium tin oxide, is held between 2 glass plates and, with the help of polarizers and deflectors, either reflects or blocks light passing through the glass. The benefits of liquid crystal displays are low cost and low voltage requirements. But they are also slow and have a very narrow viewing angle.

Keyboard Technology

The keyboard associated with a graphics workstation is often taken for granted. This is unfortunate because it is the keyboard that the operator most often uses to input data. If the keyboard is not sturdy, handy, and convenient to use, the working environment may become very uncomfortable indeed.

A number of factors should be considered when evaluating a keyboard, including the size and sensitivity of the keys and the convenience and layout of any special keypads. But first the question should be asked: is the keyboard adjustable? Ideally, keyboards should be independent from the rest of the workstation console, attached only by a single electrical cable. This allows the operator to move it easily, left or right, up or down or perhaps totally out of the way. Keyboards bolted into an immovable console are too often inconvenient and unadaptable to office environments. Modular keyboards are rapidly becoming the industry standard.

In fact, the trend in workstations has recently turned toward completely modular layouts. Each major component of the workstation—display monitor, disk drive, keyboard, tablet, cursor controller, etc.—is housed separately and connected through electrical cabling. This arrangement makes the workstation adaptable to any number of different physical environments. This versatility is particularly important as CAD/CAM technology becomes more prevalent in a greater variety of engineering, drafting, and manufacturing settings.

Other Input Devices

While the keyboard may be the most usual input device on a graphics workstation, a number of other input devices are available. One of the most common is the light pen. Light pens have been around as long as computer graphics technology (see Chapter 1) and can be exceedingly useful for inputting data as well as for directing the graphics cursor. Other cursor control devices are available as well. In addition, tablets and other digitizing devices are available to input data on a graphics system.

Light Pens

Typically, light pens are used for one of 2 purposes: either to point out graphics data already being displayed on the screen, or to position either a graphics cursor or new graphics data on the screen. On some graphics systems, light pens are used exclusively to identify choices from an on-screen menu list. Menu-driven graphics systems are most commonly used in the mechanical and manufacturing industries. On systems applied to drafting and engineering tasks, the light pen is likely to be used to identify coordinate positions when drawing lines or when inserting graphics primitives. Sometimes the pens are useful for simply positioning the cursor and making a specified point current.

Light pens are shaped like a common stylus and made to fit comfortably in one hand like a pencil. The first light pens consisted of a fiber optic bundle that transmitted light emanating from the screen back to a photomultiplier tube which, in turn, sent the information to the controller and into main memory for analysis. More recent light pens operate in exactly the opposite direction. The light pen itself issues light to the screen through a photocell. When the pen is pointed at the surface of the screen, a tracking mechanism identifies the position of the light source and records it. That point then becomes the current active position of the graphics cursor.

Cursor Control Devices

The graphics cursor is a point, cross, block of light, or set of intersecting crosshairs identifying the current working position on the graphics screen. The cursor can be moved to specified positions using various graphics software commands, or by using any of a number of hardware devices. The joystick is one example. By manipulating an upright stick left or right, up or down, the cursor is made to move accordingly on the screen. Some joysticks even permit movement in 3 dimensions: depth is controlled by twisting the stick clockwise to represent an increasing Z value and counterclockwise to represent a decreasing Z value. The values are recorded through 2 or 3 analog potentiometers that generate voltages corresponding to display screen positions. Usually the potentiometers do not have stops; therefore, when the cursor runs past one edge of the screen, it immediately appears again on the opposite screen edge.

The operating principles are much the same for a number of other graphics cursor control devices. Among these are thumbwheels corresponding to the X, Y, and Z axes; a freely rotating rollerball or trackball; a "mouse" that sits on wheels and can be pushed along a tabletop or other surface; a touchpad that responds to the pressure of a finger placed on its surface; or, even, twistable knobs. In all of these cases, the absolute position of the device is irrelevant to the cursor position; only the relative motion of the controlling device moves the cursor. Therefore, the device should be chosen according to its convenience for the user and not based on its position on the graphics console. Here again, cursor control devices built as physically independent, modular units are generally most convenient.

In choosing a cursor control device, it is important to determine how valuable it is to be able to move the cursor in one dimension at a time. Separate knobs or wheels enable users to move the cursor in the X, Y, or Z axis while not disturbing its position in any other axis. Rollerballs and joysticks make these independent movements more difficult.

It is also useful for these devices to be equipped with an incremental mode switch with which points are recorded on a grid of predetermined increments rather than at estimated points chosen by the user with only his or her eye as a guide. Incremental mode enables more accurate input of graphics data than does manual mode.

Some of these input devices are also equipped with special purpose buttons used to trigger a variety of graphics operations. The button may determine whether a designated graphic entity is made visible, what kind of line is entered (solid, dashed, dotted, etc.), or what color is displayed. These buttons, sometimes called "input function keys" or "function keys," can be very useful for even the simplest CAD/CAM applications.

Digitizers

For CAD/CAM operations involving extensive use of straightforward drafting techniques or of menus, a more accurate, more versatile method of data input exists. It involves creating an electrostatic representation of the display screen, called a "digitizer," which may have its own light pen or mouse. Small digitizers (less than 18 inches on a side) are often called "tablets," but the principle is the same. They allow users to input data without having to rely on the graphics screen. The monitor is then used more for reference or simply to confirm graphics input. The result is more accurate, cleaner data than are usually input with a graphics cursor control device and screen alone.

Much in the same way that the standard light pen uses the display screen to input or choose data, the digitizer and pen is most often used to create drawings or to operate menus. In the first case, a drawing can be input by simply using the stylus or mouse on the surface of the digitizer or by tracing a hard copy of a drawing that has been spread over the digitizer's surface. The device recognizes which points are being indicated and translates the coordinates into digital data understood by the graphics system. The graphics data are then drawn on the screen. In the second case, a menu overlay is taped down over the digitizer. Various positions on the menu correspond to stored programs or macrocommands that automatically execute when the positions are pointed out by the stylus. In this way, a series of commands can be executed with a touch, and a long series of keyboard input is avoided.

Menu Overlays

Menu overlays can be built to service a host of different applications. Most CAD/CAM vendors have a variety of menus that can be purchased as options or as part of established software applications packages. The value of good menus cannot be overestimated. They can be enormous time savers and are likely to have a significant impact on overall system productivity. Generally, the fewer the keystrokes, the faster the operator is able to work.

Most CAD/CAM system users find it beneficial to construct their own menus which automate portions of their day-to-day system operations. This is in addition to any menus originally purchased with the system. It is only common sense to take advantage of what a computer does best: repetition. Any tasks that can be automated will make the system more valuable. An adequate return on investment depends in large part on overall system productivity, not just on the ability of CAD/CAM to extend existing production tasks. In other words, the system should not only allow the customer to do what could not be done before, but to do what has always been done—only much faster.

Menu Pads

Very often on new graphics workstations, menu pads are built right into the workstation console. These pads are not really digitizers, although the technology is very similar. Rather, they consist of rows and columns of pressure sensitive buttons that can be activated by the touch of the operator's finger. Acetate overlays are made which fit over these buttons and identify the processes associated with each. Different overlays represent different sets of automated functions. Many systems are automated to the point where the system recognizes, without prompting but based on digital information imprinted on the overlay, which overlay is being used. The correct menu functions are activated instantly and without time consuming user intervention. By doing this, systems can allow users to operate a variety of menus, perhaps even swapping back and forth between them, while constructing a single drawing.

Menus are not a luxury; they are a necessity on modern CAD/CAM systems. Systems on which menus are difficult to use or to create should be regarded with skepticism.

Scanners

Optical scanners have been widely used in word processing. They identify characters typed onto a page. The characters are then stored on the word processing system for later reference or modification. Whole pages of text can be scanned in seconds. This process is obviously much faster than retyping the page on the word processor keyboard. This technology has been applied to graphics with limited success.

The first graphics scanners were able to take a drawing from the page and translate it into raster data the graphics system could understand and display. The problem has been that the data could not be modified. The displayed drawing was nothing more than an array of pixel information that made no sense to the system as vector graphics data. The usefulness of this kind of scanning is very limited.

More recently scanners are being developed that actually produce vector data that can be stored as graphics files for later reproduction or modification. This technology is very new, and, so far, expensive and very compute-intensive, but it looks promising. It is obviously must easier to scan a drawing for which only a hard copy exists, than to reproduce the drawing on-line using CAD/CAM drafting techniques. As a method of data input, scanning is likely to become very important in the near future.

Voice Recognition Systems

Another input device that completely does away with any kind of physical intervention is the voice recognition device. The operator does not have to strike a key or push a button or move a joystick or pen—he or she merely speaks into a microphone. These devices can be programed to recognize hundreds of commands. When each word is uttered the command is executed automatically. Voice recognition systems are a fast and easy way to input data, and at a starting price of less than $1000, they are very economical.

They are not without drawbacks, however. Voice recognition systems require the operator to wear a cumbersome headset that can often be uncomfortable. Moreover, they require the user to utter commands in exactly the same way each time. On occasion, they can be inadvertently activated by outside noises.

Nevertheless, these devices, by freeing up the operators hands, have many valuable applications. One of the most common is in manufacturing quality control. Inspectors can identify faulty parts by voice commands while they are holding the parts in both hands.

Specialized Workstation Hardware

The variety in graphics workstation design extends beyond variations in appearance and in display technology. The intelligence now being built into workstations also takes many forms. Some workstations are totally independent and have their own central processing unit built right into the cabinetry. Others are capable of only selective processing tasks. When choosing a workstation, the value of these hardware options should be examined closely. Some examples follow.

Displaying complex drawings can be one of the most time-consuming tasks in CAD/CAM processing. A simple pan and zoom function, for instance, requires 40 machine instructions on DEC's VAX computers. A three-dimensional rotation requires 150 instructions. More complicated displays raise the number of instructions required exponentially.

Antialiasing (i.e., any process intended to reduce the distracting visual effects of aliasing, so that stair-step lines are made to appear straight and unbroken) requires 3200 machine instructions; shading requires 8000. Hidden surface removal, a common function in most CAD/CAM applications, requires an overhead of 10,000 instructions—and the most complicated display functions, such as light source shading, require more than 20,000 machine-level processing intructions.[1] The operator could go on an extended coffee break in the time it takes many of these operations to conclude.

One solution is specially built display enhancement hardware. One of the first companies to apply the idea to CAD/CAM was Manufacturing and Consulting Services (MCS), Inc. In 1982 they announced the conversion to microcode of such display functions as pan and zooms, character generation, and menu displays. More recently, developments in very large scale integration (VLSI) chip technology (wherein more than 100,000 circuits are contained within a single chip), now permit algorithms for complex geometries to be imprinted directed onto the chip. This completely eliminates the need for microcode translations. Shaded images, and other compute-intensive display tasks can be updated much faster now than could ever be done when only software algorithms were applied to the tasks. Many CAD/CAM vendors are beginning to explore the possibilities of these kinds of hardware developments. Megatek Corporation, for example, has come out with a specially equipped graphics terminal that updates complex geometries between 5 and 15 times per second.

These and other similar hardware developments have dramatically increased CAD/CAM processing speeds. In some instances, the results border on the miraculous. As an example, hidden surface operations for complex graphics images can take up to 30 minutes when performed by software on a supermini-computer such as the VAX11/780. When that software is converted to hardware chips, the same algorithm can conclude in less than one second.[2] Given this kind of dramatic improvement in processing speed, it behooves customers interested in computer intensive applications to explore the possibilities presented by special purpose display hardware.

Among the special hardware alternatives worth looking at are tiling engines that conduct very fast surface shading algorithms, specially designed boards for pan and zoom functions, floating point processing, and solid modeling. Also of interest are hardware solutions for rotation and mirroring functions, hidden line removal, and light source shading among many others.

Other Output Devices

Output devices were among the first hardware components to be applied to graphics applications. They are also among the most useful because they make CAD/CAM data portable. Plots, films, and other types of hard copy are much easier to bring to meetings, job sites, and classrooms than display devices. The versatility of hard copy output makes these devices indispensible for most CAD/CAM applications.

Plotters

No good substitute exists for a drafting pen plotter. None of the alternatives—ink jet, electrostatic, laser transfer, impact dot matrix—as yet provides the quality, versatility, or price performance of pen plotting. For computer drafting applications, pen plotting is the best method for outputting hardcopy graphics data.

Pen plotters fall into 3 distinct categories: flatbed plotters, drum plotters, and paper movers. All of them draw lines by combining pen movements in both the X and Y axis to create lines in those 2 dimensions. Curved lines are created through a combination of movement in both axes. The pens can be ball point, felt tip, or free flowing.

Flatbed plotters have been around longer than any other type. They consist of a horizontal tabletop, on which the printed media is held down by vacuum or some mechanical means and a pen carriage device. The carriage is mounted on a mechanically controlled bar that can traverse the length of the table. Flatbed plotters are good for large plots, but the size of the table makes them hard to house, and the number of mechanical parts makes them prone to breakdowns.

Drum plotters are built more upright and the carriage bar is stationary. The paper is rolled back and forth on a drum when drawing along the vertical axis while the pen holder moves along the bar when drawing the horizontal axis. The paper can be mounted in rolls, making it possible to produce a number of plots consecutively without changing paper. They are usually smaller than flatbed plotters, however, and make the production of very wide plots impossible.

By contrast, paper mover plotters hold the printed media between 2 pinch wheels that roll the material back and forth to create vertical pen movement. The pen carousel sits on the top of the device and moves back and forth to draw the horizontal lines. Pinch wheels are lighter and faster than a drum and can be controlled with a smaller, less expensive motor. Paper-mover plotters are also more compact than other types and can be used in very small office areas without difficulty. The convenience and low price of these plotters has made them very popular in recent years, despite the limitation they place on the size of plots that can be made.

Most modern plotters possess some local intelligence. They have their own microprocessor boards that generate the plot data required to produce a drawing. The plot data are derived from device driver software residing on the host computer. Host plotter software is usually provided by the CAD/CAM vendor. This becomes the interface between the graphics system and the plotter's internal device language.

As yet, there is little standardization among device languages. Every plotter manufacturer has a unique command language. In an effort to get around this problem, plotter vendors are starting to supply standard device driver subroutines that permit plots to be defined according to coordinate positions and standard symbol definitions. This makes it easier to write the device driver software. In any case, customers should keep in mind that a plotter is only as good as the host software that drives it; reliable plotter hardware is not enough. The hardware is easier to evaluate, however. Good pen plotters should be expected to plot with a resolution of .001 inches. Accuracy should be within .004 inches. Pen speed should be variable up to about 20 inches per second. Multipen plotters should have at least 4 pens; 6 or 8 pens is usually preferable.

Other Hard Copy Devices

The alternatives to pen plotters, while cheaper, can be very unsatisfactory and should be chosen with care. Ink jet plotters, for instance, spray ink onto the paper, and while they are often cheaper than pen plotters they have a tendency to be messy, wasting both ink and paper. But this technology is improving, and the newest ink jet systems have very good resolution, are quiet, and can be used to create plots with up to 256 colors.

Impact printers create images in the same way standard typewriters create characters. They use ink ribbons of several colors which are struck from behind by tiny, needle-like hammers. The image is created in dot matrix form. Some of these printers are equipped with built-in vector-to-raster convertors which make them very good in situations where alphanumeric data are being printed at the same time as graphics data. The drawback to impact printers is relatively low resolution.

Electrostatic plotters employ digitizer technology to make plots. These devices use small electrodes which run along the length and width of the plotting area. The electrodes deliver electrical charges to a special charge retaining paper. The paper passes through an oppositely charged toner in which dots of color are attracted to the paper to create the image. These plotters are very fast and produce high quality hard copies, but as yet they are very large and expensive.

Lasers printers and thermal transfer printers are still untested newcomers to the market. They use heat to melt dots of pigment from an ink sheet which is pressed against the paper. Xerox Corporation is about the only vendor offering these printers although newer, start-up companies are beginning to appear with this technology. So far these printers are too expensive and the printing surfaces too small to make them practical in CAD/CAM applications.

Film Recorders

One other area of graphics data output deserves special mention. Film recordings of images displayed on a high-resolution graphics screen have proven to be useful and of surprisingly good quality. Quick prints and slides made directly from the CRT screen have become particularly valuable in business and presentation graphics applications.

The most common and least expensive method of reproducing screen images on film is simply to take a picture of the screen with a specially adapted camera. Usually the camera is mounted on a tripod or affixed to a hood that fits over the face of the screen. In either case the hood is necessary to block out ambient light and to hold the camera securely in place for long exposures.

A number of vendors sell both cameras and hoods that are specially built to take screen shots. The hard copy results are good enough for most presentation purposes despite several drawbacks. For one, the color representations are sometimes innacurate because of film insensitivities. For another, the curved face of the CRT screen causes slight distortions in the image, particularly around the edges. For still another, the workstation is out of production during the time the camera is being set up and the photographic exposures are taken.

These drawbacks can be overcome by spending a little extra money on additional equipment. For example, several vendors are now offering film recorders for use on specially adapted monochromatic displays. These display are programed to separate the red, blue, and green signals of an image and to display them separately. A fixed camera is focused on the screen with a color filter fitted in between. The filter is adjusted to accommodate the red, blue, and green displays individually, and the film is exposed 3 separate times, one for each color. The result is very accurate color separations and high quality pictures.

There are other film recording alternatives as well. Sophisticated laser scanners are on the market that produce both slides and prints of on-screen graphics displays. Digital devices are also available which compensate for the variations in brightness on the screen that so often distort pictures taken with conventional cameras. Other devices convert video signals directly into printable form by automatically creating 4-color separations of the on-line video data. Film recording technology, in fact, has progressed to the point that it has actually surpassed the resolutions and accuracy available in CRT design. In the future, as film recording technology grows cheaper, it will become one of the predominant methods of producing hard copies from installed CAD/CAM systems.

On-Line Data Storage

On-line data storage for CAD/CAM systems is no different from storage on any other kind of data processing system. Magnetic disks and tapes are still the standard storage media throughout the computer industry. Detailed information about their use can be found in any good text on general data processing techniques. Therefore, the discussion here will be brief.

Storage Disks

Magnetic disks come in many sizes and forms, but the basic technology is always much the same. They consist of one or more magnetic platters that spin around a central spindle. Digital data

are written to or read from the platter with a moveable head that
floats just above the magnetic surface.

Small, so-called "floppy disks," are useful on single-station
CAD/CAM systems and are often built right into the workstation
cabinetry. These disks commonly store up to 1.2 million characters and are very convenient for transferring data from one system
to another. (They are also small enough and sufficiently durable to
be sent by the mail.)

Mid-sized disks (less than 200 megabytes) are also being built
into the workstation cabinetry and are particularly useful on
single-station systems or stand-alone workstations. Disk drives
based on the new Winchester technology are often used in this
context because of their reduced size and speed.

Large disks are usually housed in their own, free-standing
drivers. They comprise a number of separate platters and can
store up to a billion characters or more. These large disks can store
thousands of drawings which may then be accessed by users
throughout a large CAD/CAM facility; they are useful in production settings requiring a large number of drawings to be on-line
simultaneously.

Disk storage requirements vary greatly between applications
and depend largely on the way a system is managed. Some system
managers may want all their graphics data on-line at the same
time; some may want to restrict access to certain disks; some may
require all users to control and maintain their own disks independently. These and related issues should be resolved before the final
system configuration requirements are settled.

Magnetic Tape Drives

Magnetic tapes also come in a variety of shapes and sizes
including everything from high-speed minicassettes to 2400-foot
reels of 1/2-inch tape that can store millions of characters. Data
are recorded on the tape as magnetic spots written along 9 parallel
recording channels. Each magnetic spot equals one bit; one complete row of 9 bits equals one byte (8 data bits and one parity bit).
Most recorders process data on tape at a density of 800 or 1600
bytes per inch (bpi), although tape drives are available that operate up to a density of 6,250 bytes per inch.

Magnetic tape is most commonly used for data transfer or for
creating back-up copies of valuable on-line data. Tape is inexpensive, dependable, and durable if stored properly. Therefore, it is a

good medium for creating system archives or for storing off-line data that is used infrequently.

Here again, the number and type of magnetic tape drives required for a CAD/CAM installation varies in relation to the way the system is managed. It is dangerous, however, not to have at least one tape drive available; without a tape drive, operators may end up with no way of transferring data to or receiving data from other systems that rely heavily on magnetic tape equipment.

References

1. Edward L. Busick, "CAD/CAM Workstation Trends," *Computer Graphics World* 7 (4) (April 1984): 60.

2. John K. Krouse, "Paperless Engineering: From Concept to Finished Part in the Computer," *Machine Design* 56 (July 12, 1984): 59.

Additional Reading

Bliss, F.W., and Hyman, G.M. "Selecting and Implementing a Turnkey Graphics System." *IEEE Computer Graphics and Applications* (April, 1981): 55-70.

Edwards, Brian J. "Dynamic Alternatives to the Keyboard." *Hardcopy* 13 (10) (October 1984): 34-44.

Ritchie, G.J. and Turner, J.A. "Input Devices for Interactive Graphics." *International Journal of Man-Machine Studies* 7 (1975): 6 39-60.

Chapter 4
Ergonomics

Few situations exist where an employee's working environment has a greater impact on performance than when that employee is working with a computer terminal. That terminal forms not only the physical environment in which that employee works, but supplies all the development tools, all the production mechanisms, and most of the avenues of communication available to the employee while at work. If the terminal is not comfortable and convenient to use, work performance naturally diminishes.

The term "ergonomics" is especially applicable here because it implies all aspects of physical and psychological comfort in the working environment. The term derives from the Greek word "ergon" meaning "work" and refers to the study of the physical relationship between humans and their working environment. The term is often applied more specifically to the study of effectively fitting production equipment to the physical and behavioral characteristics of workers. These studies are frequently used to evaluate the design of CAD/CAM systems.

Graphics Workstation Design

Let us assume a computer graphics workstation consists of 3 primary components: the display screen, the keyboard, and the working surface. Each of these components must be designed to facilitate both functionality and ease of use.

A number of workstation design requirements have already been identified and accepted as general standards. For instance, the keyboard should be detachable and must slope no more than 15 and no less than 8 degrees. The display screen must swivel and tilt, must be capable of producing high resolution images, must have an anti-glare screen, and should have easily accessible controls. The working surface must be large enough to hold architectural drawings but not so large as to be cumbersome to reach or to move. It should have a wrist support beneath the keyboard. The associated furniture must be fully adjustable and the ambient lighting, temperature, and noise levels must stay within reasonable limits. These are the kinds of obvious but important issues that must be evaluated when purchasing or designing a graphics workstation. A recent study by the National Institute for Occupational Safety and Health (NIOSH) revealed that data entry workers increased their productivity by 23% when given ergonomically designed computer terminals to work with.[1] This is a significant statistic—especially when considering the ergonomic design of the new terminals accounted for no more than preventing overhead glare, viewing angles, and adjustable keyboards and chairs.

The importance of these ergonomic considerations cannot be overstated. They figure prominently in overall worker performance. Job performance is a direct function of individual behavior, and behavior is dependent upon individual ability and level of effort. But no amount of ability or effort can overcome the physical and psychological barriers thrown up by an inhospitable work environment. And if a worker's environment consists primarily of a computer workstation, that workstation had better be suited to meet the operator's physical and psychological needs.

Workstations and Operator Psychology

A number of behavioral characteristics have been identified that directly influence individual performance on the job. Among these are perception, learning, and motivation.[2] Workstation design can affect all of these behavioral characteristics in system operators and therefore can have an enormous impact on an operator's job performance. By making that impact a positive one, both the employee and the employer will realize considerable benefits. These behavioral characteristics are described in more detail below.

Perception. Perception is a complicated process that bridges the gap between ourselves and the world around us. We receive all manner of stimuli all the time which serve to determine how we view the world. The translation of what we receive through our senses into what we accept with our understanding is called perception. Therefore, it is a 2-part process: first we accept input, and second we analy ze the input according to our own particular perspectives. The way we each react to our perceptions results in our specific patterns of behavior.

This analysis is directly applicable to judging quality in graphics workstation design. For instance, in a situation where system operators receive stimuli which distract them from the operation of the workstation, the result is behavior not conducive to work. If the lighting is bad, or the noise of an automatic printer is too loud, or if the work surface is too low, a perception is likely to be fostered that judges this an inadequate working environment. Working in such a situation and according to such a perception is very likely to give an operator a headache, backache, and eyestrain—a situation unlikely to produce good performance.

Learning. The issues of ergonomics are not limited to computer hardware. They encompass the total workstation environment including the ease with which the system can be used and the speed with which it can be learned. Much of this is tied up in the software design. Are the on-line messages clear and useful? Are the prompts accurate, concise, and professional? Are error messages positive rather than remonstrative in tone? Are all the appropriate software tools available and do they work? And, most important, is the resulting working environment conducive to learning?

Graphics workstation operators are usually interested in learning techniques or ideas that will serve to make their jobs easier. The workstation itself must be designed with this in mind. As the employee grows more familiar with the workstation, he or she must become assured of the dependability and of the accuracy inherent in the equipment. This in turn affects the behavior of the operator.

Learning tends to have a long-lasting effect on behavior; therefore, it is important that the graphics workstations be designed such that what is learned is positive and reinforces behavior that increases working performance. The workstation should allow the operator to learn how to do his or her job better and more efficiently by asking the right questions, by automatically supplying all useful information, by updating data consistently, and by reinforcing correct input rather than by failing after incorrect input or by otherwise not forgiving operator errors.

A workstation designed so that operators find their use conducive to learning is often termed "user-friendly." This means more than having polite error messages. It means all the standard operations a user is likely to encounter are truly easy to conduct. There are a number of things to look for when making this kind of evaluation, but a simple checklist would include the following:

1. Is it easy to log on?
2. Are the help messages both sufficent and clear?
3. Is there minimal variation from traditional aspects of the profession (such as vocabulary and standard units, etc.)?
4. Is the command structure logical and mnemonic?
5. Are there 2 or more levels of prompts for operators of different experience levels?
6. Is the display format easy to read?
7. Are system maintenance procedures simple to conduct?
8. Is the accompanying documentation clear and complete?

Motivations. Positive perceptions and an environment conducive to learning will go a long way toward increasing job satisfaction. Satisfaction with one's job and working environment are related directly to improved job performance—the general overall goal of both employee and employer.

Employees who find themselves in such a positive situation are an asset. Their positive attitude results in superior performance and management must work hard to retain the services of such employees. Management accomplishes this by motivating its people and keeping them interested in staying with the company. Motivation is a complicated business, but aspects of it can be built into the design of graphics workstations.

According to a survey recently conducted by Auto-trol Technology Corporation, 85% of graphics workstation operators are dedicated rather than casual users.[3] That is, 85% of these operators spend all their time working at the terminal; the output of their working day is dependent to a great extent on the workstation itself. These people are professional engineers, architects, drafters, and designers and are motivated in large part by the objective of doing the best job possible. A well designed workstation is an essential part of realizing that objective.

The workstation should maximize the number and the power of the design tools it can offer an operator. The workstation manufacturers should keep in mind that the primary benefits of their products lie in helping operators visualize their ideas. Initial drawings and subsequent revisions can all be displayed on the screen for analysis. This aids the operator in refining ideas and in determining whether they are feasible. A workstation that in any way hinders this visualization will also retard operator motivation.

Additional System Design Features

In fact, any features of a CAD/CAM system that are poorly designed, such as screen arrays, prompts, or menu functions, can be as hindering to the operator's mind as an uncomfortable chair can be to his body. Ergonomics extends not just to the worker's physical attributes and limitations, but to his or her intellectual capabilities. For instance, people do not have unlimited attention spans; therefore, processing tasks done on a graphics workstation must be fast and must be accompanied by system responses that keep the operator occupied. In addition, since operators are reluctant to read long, involved technical manuals, systems should be designed with as much on-line documentation as possible. In this way operators can become productive with the system almost immediately and are less likely to become discouraged by their progress.

Another limitation facing operators is the inability to recall without error such crucial information as file names, passwords, command syntax, and logical pathways. Here again, the system can make up for this through the use of on-line record keeping and automatic reminders. These notes will help users remember what files are where, what processing transpired during the previous day or week or month, and what work remains to be done on a specific project or set of projects.

In all of this it is important to be aware of what people do best and of what computer systems do best—and then to combine those capabilities to best advantage. Computers have excellent memories and data organizational skills; operators have excellent creative and intuitive skills. Computers thrive on repetitive tasks; operators thrive on variety. Computers maintain single levels of performance; operators work at an uneven pace but sometimes reach a level of brilliance unattainable by machines. Computers are never distracted; operators can associate disparate ideas. By combining these various skills—all of them, in some context, useful—CAD/CAM systems can be made much more efficient and effective tools than they ever could before such ergonomic issues were considered in their design.

More than anything, ergonomics is a matter of common sense. The object is to create a system—including both hardware and software—that is convenient and effective. An unused tool is no tool at all.

General Ergonomic Principles

In the most general sense, however, there are two ways of looking at ergonomics. The first is as means of eliminating hazards and inconveniences in the working environment. This principle has been applied in much of the discussion above. The second is as a means of directing the design and implementation of a working environment; that is, as a positive influence that affects the most fundamental aspects of work conditions rather than merely the superficial issues that make a poor environment more tolerable.

This latter approach to ergonomics is more difficult, but ultimately more rewarding. After all, the costs, in real dollar terms, of a poorly designed CAD/CAM system can more than offset the benefits derived from automation. These costs include low productivity, increased training time, more errors, and, more than likely, a complete overhaul and reconfiguration of the system. In other words, the liabilities of a poorly designed system may outweigh the benefits—even after ergonomic principles have been applied in an attempt to rectify problems.

Criteria for Evaluation

It is best to work from the ground up. And that is the best way to evaluate whether a given system is ergonomically sound. What then are the primary criteria for making this evaluation?

The first is simply productivity. Systems designed with ergonomic considerations in mind will be more productive than those in which the considerations were ignored. Therefore, before purchasing a CAD/CAM system, customers are advised to talk with companies that are already using the system. Ask the sales representative for the name of a reference account, somebody that has firsthand experience with the system in question. Only users can really know whether the system improved productivity ratios or not. An important point of comparison among systems is the degree of support shown them by current users.

The second criterion is quality. This concept is largely self-evident: a well designed system produces high quality results. In CAD/CAM this suggests that the system is accurate, dependable, and easy to learn and use. When CAD/CAM is implemented in any setting, product quality should naturally rise. Anything else is unacceptable.

The third criterion is satisfaction of users. The system must provide some advantage over alternative methods of production or it is of no use whatever. If CAD/CAM is a hindrance to users, the installation is in trouble. Operators want tools that make their job easier and that enhance their ability to solve problems. CAD/CAM should be expected to do that.

References

1. David Kull, "Demystifying Ergonomics," *Computer Decisions* 16 (11) (September 1984): 144.

2. Andrew D. Szilagyi and Marc J. Wallace, *Organizational Behavior and Performance,* 3d ed. (Glenview, IL: Scott, Foresman and Company, 1983), p. 234.

3. Auto-trol In-house Survey, October, 1984. Unpublished.

Additional Reading

Cakir, A.; Har, D.S.; and Stewart, T. *Visual Display Terminals.* John Wiley and Sons, New York: 1980.

Foley, James D., et al. "The Human Factors of Computer Graphics Interaction Techniques." *IEEE Computer Graphics and Applications* 4 (11) (November 1984): 13-48.

Hayes, P., et al. "Breaking the Man-Machine Communication Barrier." *Computer* 14 (3) (March 1981): 19-30.

Knapp, John M. "The Ergonomic Millennium." *Computer Graphics World* (6) (June 1983): 86-93.

McCormick, E.J. *Human Factors in Engineering and Design.* 5th ed. New York: McGraw-Hill Publishing Co. 1982.

Ohlson, M., "System Design Considerations for Graphic Input Device." *Computer* 11 (11) (November 1979): 9-18.

Chapter 5
System and Applications Software:
Guidelines for Evaluation

CAD/CAM system software is more difficult to evaluate than hardware. Inadequacies, inaccuracies, and inconsistencies in the software are very often revealed only after the system has been in use for some time. Yet it is the software, above all, that makes a CAD/CAM system accessible and useful. Potential customers, therefore, should have a clear and reasonable set of expectations which define minimum standards for software function and reliability. These expectations derive, first of all, from an understanding of how CAD/CAM system software is organized.

CAD/CAM system software generally can be divided into 3 major categories: operating systems, graphics software, and applications. These categories can usefully be viewed as a logical hierarchy with the operating system at the bottom, the graphics system in the middle, and applications on top. If we extend this hierarchy to include the operator, he or she is the outermost level and views the the system from the outside in. Operators, therefore, are closest to the applications software and farthest from the operating system. This relationship should be kept in mind as we review each category, because it affects the way in which each category must be designed.

Operating System Software

The operating system, as the lowest level in this hierarchy, controls the lowest level of system operations. It is a collection of programs that conducts all the routine, housekeeping tasks required of the computing system. These tasks can be conveniently divided into 3 categories: system controls, processing tasks, and data management.

The system control tasks include all supervision and maintenance requirements of the system. The programs conducting these tasks set job priorities, initiate and terminate processing tasks, assign devices and hardware registers, control data input and output functions, and supervise central processing unit (CPU) time.

The processing tasks, on the other hand, include language translators, service programs, and system utilities. These programs organize data, link programs, create and maintain system libraries, and translate data from one format to another. They also handle all the system utility functions which are used to sort and merge files, move data throughout the system, edit text, delete old files, conduct back-ups, and the like.

The data management programs control the organization and access of all on-line data. Most of this is done automatically, relieving the graphics system of the necessity of blocking data, indexing records, setting pointers, and otherwise formatting data storage.

In general, the more routine work that can be conducted at the operating system level, the more efficient the whole system will become. A good, solid set of operating system programs eliminates redundant programing, reduces program overhead, and eliminates many data management errors. A good graphics system depends heavily on the tools provided by the operating system on which it runs; it is written with the presumption that these tools are available and operate efficiently and without error.

Most important among these tools to the graphics operator are the language translators and the system utilities. These programs facilitate all of the graphics system management tasks. System archives and back-ups, for instance, are created by operating system utility programs activated by commands like "Save," "Back-up," and "Restore." Disk initializing and formatting tasks are conducted by activating utility programs designed for that purpose. Copying graphics files for hard copy output and conducting routine system security and file management functions are also accomplished with system utility programs.

Moreover, the implementation of language translators, such as FORTRAN, PASCAL, or C compilers, BASIC interpreters, or translators for more specialized manufacturing languages or numerical control languages, extend the graphics capabilities in the direction of a completely integrated manufacturing system.

Operating system tools of this kind enable the sophisticated CAD/ CAM system operator or manager to automate more of the responsibilities that rightly fall under the auspices of computer-aided manufacturing concepts. The need for these tools should be evaluated carefully and compared with those available on a given CAD/CAM system before the decision to purchase CAD/CAM technology is made.

Graphics System Software

The graphics system software is the keystone of any CAD/ CAM system. This group of programs, with a solid and versatile operating system to rely on, creates and manipulates the graphics data on which the application of the system depends. The graphics system is that part of the CAD/CAM system software on which the operator depends most and interacts most directly.

The architects of a graphics software system then have 2 major responsibilities: (1) to provide a complete set of graphics tools, and (2) to make those tools easily accessible to the system operator. A graphics system that does not satisfy both requirements is inadequate. There are, however, degrees to which these requirements are satisfied.

Menu-Driven vs. Command-Driven Systems

Graphics systems are generally based on one of 2 design principles: they are either menu-driven or command-driven. In the first case, a list of options is displayed on the screen from which the operator chooses. The choice is made either with a keyboard entry or, on some systems, with a light pen pointed at the menu screen. Each choice entails its own set of additional displayed options in a continuing chain of logical branches that each culminate in a single graphics processing function. In the second case of command-driven systems, by contrast, the final command is entered directly into the system and executed immediately.

Menu-driven systems are easier for the novice to learn. The commands are displayed on the screen along with a brief explanation of each so that choosing the correct command requires no memorization or prior knowledge. These systems are, however, slower than command-driven systems—especially if each menu choice is entered at the keyboard rather than directly off the screen as with a light pen. It takes time to paint each menu on the screen and to process each choice. Graphics functions requiring the user to run through a whole series of menus can be very time consuming indeed. Therefore, menu-driven graphics systems should be equipped with several different levels of operation.

The first level is for novice users and lists complete menus on the screen as well as descriptions or other "help" messages clarifying those menus. The second level is for more experienced users and may display abbreviated menus without elaborate explanation on the assumption that the user is beyond needing such rudimentary help. Display time is thus reduced and processing speed is increased dramatically. A third level of operation is exclusively for system experts and omits all but the most essential displayed information. Minimizing display time maximizes user productivity. At the third level of operation, menu-driven systems are much faster than command-driven systems. And by allowing the user to choose the level of operation with which he or she is most comfortable, the whole system is made much more efficient. Menu-driven graphics system software without the capacity for several levels of operation are prone to inefficiencies and may contribute to operator boredom and low quality output.

Command-driven systems, on the other hand, should include a full complement of training aids. Not only should the system, as any software system, have clear and concise "help" messages and error messages, it should be supported with good documentation and training classes. Most CAD/CAM vendors will include formal instruction as part of the purchase price of the turnkey system. Customers should avail themselves of this service. Effective training and documentation can have an enormous and beneficial effect on a CAD/CAM system's overall productivity—particularly in the first year of its operation. (For a fuller discussion of training considerations, see Chapter 6.)

Moreover, the command terminology should be reasonable and consistent with drafting and engineering standards. If experienced drafters or designers find themselves, when operating the CAD/CAM system for the first time, confronting a misleading or confusing set of command names, something is wrong. Circle commands should draw circles; spline commands should draw splines. The mirror command should do exactly that—reflect the mirror image of existing graphics data. Lines should be called lines and not "vectorized axial extensions" or some other such non-sense. Be very critical of on-screen dialog—it may save aggravation later.

The Use of Icons

In an effort to make on-screen dialog more comprehensible, many systems are turning to extensive use of icons. This technique has proven efficient and its use is likely to increase. The principle behind it is simple: graphic symbols are easier to understand than text.

Iconographic systems display graphic images instead of or along with text. These images are often more compact than pure text and may even evoke meaning more clearly. For instance, an image of a trash can and a file cabinet are more succinct menu selections than an explanation of how to save or destroy files. A picture of a disk may be enough to explain how to copy a file from one place to another. An image of a pair of scissors could suggest a clipping operation.

Icons operate as do on-screens menus used to such benefit with digitizers and tablets. (See Chapter 3.) They are easy to understand and they are fast—qualities which make them significant in the eyes of potential users.

Applications Software

On top of the operating system and graphics system software lies the applications software. Applications can be run as individual software components or as an organized set of inter-dependent tools, each fulfilling a portion of the requirements defined by an integrated production plan.

Each application is specifically tailored to meet the CAD or CAM needs of a defined industry. The programs must be designed with an understanding of the standards and goals of that industry—a condition that puts considerable demands on the programers developing the software. After all, how many programers are also practicing architects, or plumbers, or electricians, or biomechanists? Good applications software is very hard to come by—and hard to pick out from among the many packages now appearing on the market.

Not unexpectedly, the best applications programs are written by experts. Experts concentrate their efforts on narrow markets. Customers should beware of CAD/CAM vendors who claim to do everything well—no one can be an expert in all application areas. The available applications options should be scrutinized carefully before a final purchasing decision is made to ensure that the applications software is both comprehensive and easy to use.

The best CAD/CAM software is now being written by small software houses who specialize. Even the large turnkey CAD/CAM vendors are beginning to realize this. Many of them, rather then trying to develop their own applications software, are buying the rights to software developed externally, or entering into joint marketing agreements with independent software manufacturers. These turnkey vendors then provide their customers access to state-of-the-art applications software through specially written interfaces. Everyone benefits.

A good way of evaluating applications software is through benchmarks. Potential customers bring to the CAD/CAM vendor a processing problem that is representative of the tasks they want their system to handle. The vendor, using a system configured similarly to the system they propose to sell this customer, does the work while the customer watches. In this way, the customer can evaluate the speed and versatility of the software firsthand and compare the results to any other benchmarks from other vendors.

What to Look for in a Benchmark

Benchmarks should not be evaluated casually. They can be as misleading as they are helpful. The objective is to produce representative results, given a representative system and representative circumstances. Allowing vendors to display their systems in the best possible circumstances will not provide much data on how that system will operate in a real production environment.

By the same token, the benchmark should not place unreasonable demands on the vendor. Exhaustive benchmark requirements may discourage some vendors from participating in the benchmark or from submitting a bid at all. The purpose of the benchmark is to allow the vendors to display their systems in an environment that will both reveal less qualified systems and highlight the most qualified systems.

During the benchmark, the customer should not be afraid to ask questions. Find out exactly what the vendor is doing on the system when satisfying the benchmark requirements. Take note of the time required to do displays and to change displays. Use a stopwatch if necessary to make comparisons. Be aware of the number of keystokes required for various operations. Numerous keystrokes take time and can add significantly to production time over the long run. Also be alert to special performance-enhancing hardware or software that will cost extra or that is not available on the system as you intend to buy it. And above all, formulate specific expectations about the quality of the output data and hold each system to those expectations. System speed is of little help if the output is of unusable quality.

CAD/CAM Applications

CAD/CAM systems are by now being applied to scores of different industries. Future applications will depend more on our collective imaginations than on the limitations of the technology. The following list of CAD/CAM applications is incomplete, but it serves to illustrate the diversity of CAD/CAM.

Advertising Layout
Air Traffic Control
Animation
Architecture
Biomechanics
Business Graphics
Cabinet Making
Chemical Engineering
Civil Engineering
Communications
Clothing Design
Data Scanning
Debugging
Decision Analysis
Demographic Analysis
Differential Equations
Drafting
Electrical Engineering

Engineering Analysis
Exploration Research
Finite Elements Analysis
Flight Simulation
Forecasting
Geophysical Research
Graphic Arts
Heating, Ventilation, Air
    Conditioning System Design
Human Factors Engineering
Industrial Design and
    Engineering
Information Management
Integrated Circuit Design
Inventory
Machine Tooling
Manufacturing Process
Monitoring and Analysis

Part Analysis	Spectrographic Analysis
Pharmacology	Statistical Analysis
Piping Design	Stress Analysis
Plant Design	Structural Analysis
Power System Design	Technical Illustration
and Monitoring	Text Editing
Printed Circuit Board Design	Radar Display and Analysis
Production Planning	Thermal Engineering
Programming	Trajectory Analysis
Publishing	Voice Studies
Siesmographics Analysis	War Game Simulation
Sheet Metal Layout	Weapons Research
Simulation	

In each of these applications, the software creates and organizes graphics data to be modified by a system operator. These 3 principles—graphics creation, data organization, and data modification—provide the basis for evaluating all applications software.

How is a Computer Drawing Created?

A turnkey CAD/CAM system then, as we have described, requires hardware, software, and an operator. How those components are used to create a drawing is a little more difficult to outline. Each component—hardware, software, operator—works as a part of the whole process. The hope is that the process remains harmonious.

Any drawing begins as an idea. We have explored the creative process entailed in producing an engineering drawing in Chapter 2. But how does it grow from an idea to a finished drawing? How does the CAD/CAM system manifest the designer's idea?

Data Input

The first step in creating a drawing is inputting the geometry. This process has not changed much in the many years since computer graphics technology was first introduced. Most data input is still done manually.

The most rudimentary way to input data is to enter the appropriate commands or a digitized description of each point and line—one element at a time. This is only one step above manual drafting and can be almost as time-consuming. Any shortcut to this method can be of great help.

Quite a number of modeling systems are now on the market that make graphics input faster. The most promising method is "procedural modeling"—using macrocommands or on-line processing procedures instead of explicit geometries. The user simply activates the modeling system and supplies appropriate responses to on-screen prompts. The geometry is then created automatically according to the predefined steps of the procedures.

In theory, a good, general purpose procedural modeling system will allow operators to build virtually any geometric construct. The reality is somewhat less than the theory, however, as it is not beyond the developmental stage. Nevertheless, it is still a very good method of creating geometric composites from graphics primitives in industries requiring a lot of repetitive drafting.

Another method of automating graphics data input is "extrusion." This method adds complexity to existing geometric entities by extrapolating from one dimension to the next. Lines are generated from points; planes from lines; and solids from planes. This method of automating data input is particularly valuable for constructs having symmetrical form.

Still another method of data input is termed "lofting." Lofting creates a system that analyzes the 2-dimensional contours of objects created manually. The system then produces cross-sections of the objects automatically in 3 dimensions. Lofting is particularly applicable to the mapping industry where topographic contours can be used to simulate three-dimensional representations of cartographic data.

Many other methods of data input are also available to CAD/CAM operators. "Patching," for instance, is an established and widely used method of creating geometric entities in sections, each one of which can be modified independently—a characteristic particularly useful in creating curved surfaces such as those required in the design of airplane bodies or automobile bumpers. Most of these methods are useful in some applications; none is likely to help everyone. Any method that automates rote data input procedures can help productivity ratios and operator motivations. But overall, the development of data input methods has lagged behind other CAD/CAM technology developments. (For more information on input devices see Chapter 3.)

Display Generation

Once the data are input, the next logical step in creating a serviceable drawing is to display it on the workstation screen. Here the geometry becomes more complex because the input data, to be comprehensible, must be displayed in the proper perspective. Three-dimensional information is being projected onto a 2-dimensional screen.

When the data are first input, they are stored in terms of a logical coordinate system understood by the system. Data must be displayed in terms of a perspective coordinate system understood by the operator. The Z axis, representing depth, is depicted by reducing the size of objects in the background, increasing the size of foreground data, and by converging lines as they recede into the distance. All of this must be done consistently and in the proper relation to the operator's field of vision; otherwise, the display will be more confusing than helpful. All good CAD/CAM systems should make this conversion automatically.

Once the projection has been defined and the data are placed in the proper perspective in relation to the operator's field of vision, the system must determine what, if any, data lie outside that field of vision. In other words, the entire graphics file may be of a size and in a perspective that will not allow all of it to be displayed without distortion. In such cases, certain data must be clipped out of the displayed image. This automatic clipping is not usually disturbing because the field of vision on most systems is made to coincide with the physical boundaries of the display screen itself.

These display operations—coordinate transformation, perspective division, and clipping—have traditionally been done with various software algorithms. More recently these operations are built into the display hardware and processed locally in the workstation itself. This latter arrangement is advantageous because it has a dramatic, positive effect on display response time. In general, hardware is faster than software.

Hidden Line Removal

After the data have been transformed and put in proper perspective they still may not make a comprehensible display if the system does not account for data that should not be visible. Some of the graphics information will be obscured from view if it lies behind a solid plane or beyond the visible portion of a curve. For the sake of visual clarity these parts of the drawing should not be displayed.

A number of algorithms exist for determining hidden lines and surfaces. All of them require considerable computational overhead. (This makes comparisons of the speed of hidden line removal functions good candidates for evaluating competing benchmarks.) Displaying the results of these computations, however, is not difficult. On calligraphic display devices, the end point for each vector is calculated and the line is turned off at that point. On raster display devices, each pixel is examined for visibility.

Additional Image Enhancement Techniques

The final touches added to a displayed drawing are what distinguish CAD/CAM systems most from manual drafting. The most sophisticated systems, in fact, can produce images that approach photographic quality. Several display techniques may be involved.

The most obvious and common image enhancement technique is adding color. Recall from Chapter 3 that most CAD/CAM workstations produce color by combining varying degrees of red, blue, and green. Color can be used to enhance a drawing by approximating the way that image might appear to the eye in the real world. It can also be used to emphasize parts of the drawing, distinguish among parts, or to color code information. (For additional discussion of the use of color see Appendix I.)

Surface shading is another way of making displayed images appear more representational. Shading simulates the transmission, absorption, or reflection of light as it strikes the surface of an object. The algorithms for surface shading account for the angle of the light source, the texture, color, and shape of the surface on which the light is directed, and for the properties and reflection geometry implied by the material from which the surface is made. As these algorithms become more sophisticated, computer-generated images will become virtually identical to photographic or handpainted images. This advanced graphics technology is already being used extensively in the film, television, and animation industries.

Still other graphics processing developments are adding to the versatility and quality of computer-generated pictures. Anti-aliasing algorithms are in use which counteract the jagged lines and stair-step effects caused by the resolution limitations of raster display screens. Software has been developed that automatically creates shadows on the screen based on the direction and intensity of ambient lighting. Shadows enhance the 3-dimensional appearance of the object on the screen and further enable operators to see and understand spatial relationships. Texturing algorithms are another example of display techniques being applied to increasing the realism of computer graphics displays. Fractal geometry, an entirely new realm of mathematical analysis developed by Dr. Benoit Mandelbrot at IBM, is being applied to computer graphics to increase the level of detailing. [1]

Other image enhancement techniques are doubtless already in the works. So are other applications software packages—and new and better graphics systems. However since CAD/CAM is already proven valuable, potential customers should not postpone the purchase of CAD/CAM just because they are waiting for better equipment to appear on the market. Such a wait is not likely to be short; a better system will always be just around the corner.

Reference

1. Susan West, "New Realism," *Science 84* 5 (6) (July/August 1984): 35.

Additional Reading

Catmull, E. "A Hidden-Surface Algorithm with Anti-Aliasing." *Computer Graphics* 12 (August 1978): 6-10.

W. Giloi, *Interactive Computer Graphics: Data Structures, Algorithms, Languages.* Englewood Cliffs, NJ: Prentice Hall, 1978.

Newman, W.M. and Sproull, R.F. *Principles of Interactive Computer Graphics.* New York: McGraw-Hill Publishing Co. 1979.

Whitted, T. "An Improved Illumination Model for Shaded Display." *Communications of the ACM* (June 1980): 343-49.

Chapter 6
Personnel and Training

Effective use of CAD/CAM technology requires that managers and operators have skills and training specific to CAD/CAM or to its application. Happily, the days are gone when CAD/CAM systems were installed and operated only by high-level computer scientists. Many universities have incorporated CAD/CAM curricula into their design, engineering, fine arts, and computer science departments. CAD/CAM operator training classes are common in industry. Systems are much more accessible now.

But with that accessibility has come an increased CAM personnel. Because CAD/CAM is being installed in all manner of industries, recruiting and maintaining the people needed to run these systems efficiently has become very competitive. Qualified people are becoming scarcer. Companies can adapt to this shortage in 2 ways: by providing additional training to existing employees, or by successfully competing for people who already have marketable CAD/CAM skills. Most analysts would agree that the first method is best—for many reasons. Chief among them is that it reduces internal dissension and that it is less expensive in the long run.

Defining Job Requirements

The most important task in finding personnel for any new department is, of course, defining the jobs that need to be filled. This sounds simple enough—but it may not be. CAD/CAM means different things to different people.

As part of the planning process for implementing CAD/CAM, it is a good idea to put a committee together whose objective is to determine personnel requirements for the impending system. This committee should consist of representatives from each of the departments that stand to benefit from the system and appropriate representatives from the personnel department. Their job is to evaluate precisely what the system is expected to do. The following set of questions must be answered to everyone's satisfaction:

1. Which departments stand to benefit from CAD/CAM?
2. Which departments will implement CAD/CAM first?
3. Who is responsible for system management?
4. How many workstations will be available initially?
5. What role (specifically) will CAD/CAM play in the company?

The next task is to evaluate the experience and skills of existing personnel in light of the above questions. If the company already has a management information system (MIS), or a data processing (DP) group, the employees working in those departments should be evaluated first, as some of them may help to implement and manage the CAD/CAM system. They may even want to include the CAD/CAM system as part of the larger data processing function and manage the technology as an integrated whole. Anyone with engineering, computer science, drafting, or designing experience should also be evaluated and questioned about his or her willingness and interest in participating in the CAD/CAM installation.

Employees most likely to have their jobs automated should be identified. They must be made aware of the likely impact CAD/CAM will have on their work. Most of them can be expected to be receptive to the idea; professionals usually welcome any tool they can use to enhance their job performance, and they can be encouraged by the fact most people can easily learn to use CAD/CAM. According to a recent survey by Daratech, Inc., a computer graphics consulting firm, most people learn adequate CAD/CAM skills within 3 months and go on to become skilled operators within 6 months. Fewer than 10% of employees introduced to CAD/CAM fail to develop marginal operator skills.[1]

Next, management must analyze the personnel requirements of the CAD/CAM system itself. This is essential to determine what kinds of skills and what levels of experience are necesary for running the system properly. It is also important to decide what kinds of career paths are available and whether to promote people from within or hire new employees for given jobs.

The following pages offer suggestions on how to classify personnel required to run a CAD/CAM facility and might be used as a basis for building a CAD/CAM department. Each position is given a title, a job description, and guidelines on the education and experience candidates should have. The jobs have to be covered by someone, no matter what the position is titled, and no matter who reports to whom—the tasks will be much the same for any CAD/CAM installation.

CAD/CAM Consultant

The first major CAD/CAM installations in American business appeared in the mid-1960s. At that time, the technology was untested and management reluctant to put up the large sums of money required to get the projects started. Usually in those cases, the impetus behind installing the systems came from one or 2 persistent advocates of CAD/CAM working within the company. This was the case at Lockheed-Georgia, General Motors, and with the first installations by the U.S. Navy.[2]

These advocates had to be experts in CAD/CAM technology—their credibility depended upon it. As unlikely as it might seem, this situation persists today. Management still tends to know little about CAD/CAM and relies on the advice of experts. The difference is that today these experts are available for hire.

Many CAD/CAM consulting firms are springing up to give advice on all manner of CAD/CAM applications. They can be very useful—especially if the company is not blessed with a CAD/CAM expert of its own. In either case, whether it is an employee or an outside expert, the role of CAD/CAM consultant is singularly important in organizing CAD/CAM related activities.

The consultant's role is to be the organizing principle for the entire CAD/CAM operation. He or she does this in several ways, primarily by leading discussions, both formal and informal, on the use of CAD/CAM and the benefits it will provide the company. In this way, he or she tries to ease reluctant employees to accept CAD/CAM. In addition, the consultant continually evaluates the progress of the installation of CAD/CAM and looks for ways to make it more efficient and more palatable to system operators—in short, to get the most that he or she can out of this technology on behalf of the company.

These responsibilities demand that the consultant be conversant both in the latest developments of CAD/CAM and in the business of the company employing it. He or she must be both manager and technologist. This combination of skills is hard to find and, therefore, the CAD/CAM consultant is likely to command a salary above $50,000 per year and report directly to the executive level of the company.

System Manager

The day-to-day management of the CAD/CAM system falls to the system manager. The responsibilities of the job include assigning processing priorities, administrating system security, determining working and maintenance schedules, and fulfilling programing requirements. This position is crucial to maintaining an efficient CAD/CAM facility.

It is usual for the system manager to report to a department or division head. In this kind of arrangement, the CAD/CAM system is an autonomous group. The system is then an arm of the engineering, drafting, or manufacturing department it has been purchased to service rather than of the data processing group or the management information services department.

An alternative to this arrangement can be considered, however. Some CAD/CAM installations are managed as though they are a part of the data processing department. In this case the system is not under the control of the people for whom it does the most work but is controlled by the data processing professionals who have considerable expertise in the areas of system integration and support—an important asset since most CAD/CAM systems eventually require integration with other computing systems. This arrangement has been made to work well in many settings, but experience has shown that the MIS/DP staff is not often equipped with the knowledge needed to understand the proper use of CAD/CAM. Therefore, this kind of system management often encounters start-up problems.

In either case, the system manager must be a computer scientist, or at least have a strong background in computing principles and in software development. This person needs to be able to do system troubleshooting, software maintenance, and to perform routine data management tasks such as archiving, disk initializing, queuing, booting, data consolidating, and the like. In addition, he or she may be required to do special programing. System managers typically have at least 5 years of experience in data processing and command salaries in the range of $30,000 to $40,000 per year.

System Programer

If the system manager does not have the time or the skill to fulfill system programing tasks, someone else must be appointed to the task. Very often this person, usually titled "System Programer," specializes in applications software.

Some system managers would consider it a luxury to have a programer on staff and assigned to the CAD/CAM department. But as applications become more complex and tailored to more specific industries, system programers are becoming more of a necessity. Most CAD/CAM installations have special, if not unique, processing requirements that are not likely to be addressed by off-the-shelf applications packages sold by most vendors. The software must be tailored to fit—and that work falls to the system programer.

System programers are computer scientists with CAD/CAM applications experience. It is also helpful if they have some understanding of system-level programing and architecture. It is most important, however, that they have a thorough understanding of the industry to which the CAD/CAM system is being applied.

Experienced system programers with expertise in specific industries are expensive. Those with less experience are happy to be placed in CAD/CAM facilities applied to the industry of their particularly interest. Therefore, salaries for system programers can vary widely, perhaps as much as between $25,000 and $50,000 per year including incentive bonuses.

System Operators

The system operators are those who spend the bulk of their day sitting in front of a CAD/CAM workstation. They are the engineers, designers, drafters, illustrators, architects, etc., who use the system daily and for whom the system has provided automation in their work.

System operators may have CAD/CAM experience, but that is certainly not a requirement of the job. Primarily, they are skilled at specific technical tasks that can be handled by CAD/CAM applications. If they know nothing about CAD/CAM, they can learn. And obviously it is much more efficient to teach an architect to use CAD/CAM than it is to teach a CAD/CAM expert to be an architect. Casual knowldge or even ignorance of CAD/CAM should be no impediment to anyone wanting to be a system operator.

Most system operators will come from within the company. They already have the expertise in their jobs that makes them valuable assets. By automating this expertise they will become even more valuable. A properly installed CAD/CAM system will not displace anyone currently in the company who is willing to learn.

Training

Virtually all CAD/CAM vendors offer some sort of training. The training can be one- or 2-week formal seminars with hands-on practice, a series of shorter seminar sessions spread over longer time periods, on-line computer-aided instruction, or even self-teaching manuals. In each of these situations, the goal is really twofold: to teach operators how to use the system, and to create a working climate in which the potential of CAD/CAM can be realized. A good training program will do wonders in convincing operators of the value of CAD/CAM and in making it acceptable to existing employees.

The best training classes are highly organized, relatively formal, classes taught by professional instructors at off-site locations. In such settings there are fewer distractions and the atmosphere is more conducive to learning. Ideally the classwork is divided evenly between lecture/demonstration and hands-on practice sessions. It is very important, therefore, that classrooms be equipped with working graphics terminals. A ratio of one terminal for 2 students is sufficient to give everyone time to practice working on the system. Any fewer terminals presents problems because there is no real substitute for hands-on experience with the equipment.

Most good vendor training programs will offer a variety of classes. Some vendors offer separate courses for managers and applications programers as well as system operators. When undertaking initial training classes, customers are well-advised to schedule classes as close as possible to the time their system is being installed. Students should be able to return from training and go immediately to work without waiting through an interim period during which learned skills can be easily forgotten.

The basic operator training class provides an introduction to standard operating functions including start-up and shutdown, using peripheral devices, and conducting routine preventive maintenance. Most of the class, however, is devoted to learning basic graphics functions such as file creation and modification, use of menus, graphics command structures, text insertion, rotation, and dimensioning. By the end of this class, students should be able to create rudimentary drawings and have an understanding of general system operations.

After operators have completed preliminary training and had several months of additional experience, it is often a good idea to follow up with an advanced training course. This course entails instruction on advanced drafting methods and standard applications packages such as bill of material, coordinate geometry, report generators, procedural modeling, or finite element analysis. After this kind of advanced training and perhaps several more months of experience, operators can be expected to be proficient in the use of their CAD/CAM system. Those employees who are not progressing will be a distinct minority.

Other training classes can also be of great practical value. Particularly important are courses on system management. These classes address not only system implementation and maintenance issues, but such issues as hiring, productivity analysis, bonus and incentive plans, ergonomics, and system upgrades. Some other classes of note: applications training classes, which teach about the use of specialized applications software, and CAD/CAM programing techniques, which teach operators how to use specialized manufacturing languages to enhance productivity and further automate ther jobs.

Most of all, however, training is an essential part of preparing for an orderly transition to CAD/CAM. It is a way to convince employees of the benefits of CAD/CAM and how it will enhance their jobs rather than diminish them. Most experienced CAD/CAM users already know that CAD/CAM improves working conditions   offices are remodeled to accomodate the new equipment, job descriptions are upgraded (sometimes coincident with salary increases), training programs are enhanced, opportunities for advancement increase, and many of the rote tasks previously done by hand will be automated. CAD/CAM training, in preparing for these changes, has a way of improving morale.

References

1. Charles M. Foundyller, "The Psychology of CAD/CAM," *Design Graphics World* 8 (7) (July 1984): 8-15.

2. Donald Greenberg *The Computer Image: Applications of Computer Graphics* (Reading, MA: Addison-Wesley Publishing Co., 1982) p. 8.

Additional Reading

Dunn, Robert M. and Herzog, Bertram, consulting eds. *CAD/CAM Management Strategies.* Pennsauken, NJ: Auerbach Publishers Inc., 1984.

Green, R. Elliot and Parslow, R.D., eds. *Computer Graphics in Management: Case Studies of Industrial Applications.* New York: Auerbach Publishers, Inc., 1970.

Hegland, Donald E. "CAD/CAM—Key to the Automatic Factory." *Production Engineering* (August 1981): 31-35.

Chapter 7
Justification and Evaluation in Business

Technical innovation by itself is not enough to justify CAM. Just because CAD/CAM can be useful does not mean it will be.

We have already explored how CAD/CAM technology tends to integrate various aspects of design and manufacturing and how it is the beginning of a move toward computer-integrated manufacturing (CIM). Yet, for the most part, that move is just a beginning and we are a long way from the completely automated factories science fiction writers have been portending.

Much of the difficulty in implementing CAD/CAM goes beyond the limitations of the technology. It can be found in the organization. People in business are notoriously reluctant to change. They seem to believe that their jobs depend on maintaining the status quo. Most CAD/CAM installations fail for sociological rather than technological reasons.

One expert in CAD/CAM has written, in apparent exasperation, "The business organization is a wonderful, but poorly understood, living entity that shares with other complex organisms a first-order predilection for survival. And, just as the human body resists rearrangement of its organs and functions, so most businesses resist changes. They are resisted not for their precise nature, but *because* they are changes."[1] This intractable attitude is very difficult to overcome when trying to justify the purchase and implementation of CAD/CAM. Yet by not overcoming it, the installation is doomed to failure.

Planning

The best way to proceed when justifying a CAD/CAM system is through careful, long-term planning. Long-term plans may seem an exercise in futility to professional people who are used to seeing business plans change daily, but without them it is very difficult to contend successfully with the innate resistence to change in corporate organizations.

In the case of CAD/CAM, where the change implied is wholesale, planning must be very long term indeed. Many CAD/CAM consultants suggest drawing plans that set 5- and 10-year milestones. This kind of long-term planning can have several beneficial effects. It is an indication to employees that the company's commitment to CAD/CAM is strong. It also aids management in arriving at realistic expectations for this technology. And long-term plans provide a measure against which the ultimate success or failure of the installation can be judged; in such a context, minor setbacks are less likely to be mistaken for major ones.

When making these plans, it is important to set high goals. Allow CAD/CAM technology the freedom to live up to its potential. Instead of aiming for productivity increases of 20%, aim for 200%. Assume that CAD/CAM can be made to permeate all phases of the production environment.

The following productivity improvement ratios are reasonable, even conservative, goals to shoot for in the industries specified.

Industry	Productivity Gain
Mechanical	5:1
Architectural	7:1
Piping	5:1
Structural	5:1
Electrical	7:1
Production Engineering	6:1
Graphic Arts	8:1
Mapping	60:1
Civil Engineering	8:1
General Drafting	10:1[2]

Impediments to Measuring CAD/CAM Benefits

When developing these long-term plans, it is often difficult or impossible to quantify the benefits of CAD/CAM in a way that management can understand. Traditional methods of measuring the cost benefits are inadequate because they concentrate too closely on the immediate effects of a CAD/CAM system. Faster production is only part of the story because it ignores such cost improvements as shorter design cycles and better product quality.

Moreover, CAD/CAM tends to reduce expensive errors otherwise encountered during product design, such as building inadequate mock-ups or sending to production parts requiring unrealistic tolerances. Traditional accounting methods cannot measure these kinds of cost reduction benefits. It is very difficult to describe accurately, for instance, the amount of money saved when a product design is thoroughly analyzed by automatic rather than manual means. Too many considerations are likely to be left out, including the relative accuracy obtainable by each method, the ease of manufacture built into the design, and the prudent use of available or standard materials.

Benefits That Can Be Measured

The important thing to be remembered when outlining the cost benefits of CAD/CAM is that they are far-reaching. Look for the big things that stand out against the horizon, rather than the little things in the foreground that may be numerous but do not add up to much.

Shortened Design Cycles

The most obvious (and easiest to quantify) benefit to CAD/ CAM is speed. Design, drafting, and manufacturing projects take less time to complete with CAD/CAM than they would without it. The savings resulting from this benefit alone can be enormous. Time saved is money found: operators produce more per hour, money borrowed to finance projects can be paid back sooner, reducing interest payments, and, most important of all, speed may result in the acquisition of additional job contracts that can be worth a great deal of money in the future.

Improved Staff Skills

Another measurable benefit to CAD/CAM is the improvement in the level and variety of skills possessed by the operating staff. Operators will have the opportunity to learn to work with new tools and sharpen their existing skills with the help of those tools. They also can branch out into new fields such as database management, system management, software development, group technology, inventory control, job accounting, and all the other tasks that can be automated by a full-function CAD/CAM installation, so career path opportunities are broadened. All of these things tend to produce employees who are happier, more productive, and more versatile.

Better Product Quality

CAD/CAM always improves product quality. This, in turn, translates into savings on several fronts. Scrap materials, retooling, and warranty costs are held to a minimum. Product quality assurance inspections are reduced in direct proportion to the lessened probability of finding defects. The quantity of parts that must be produced to satisfy lot size requirements is significantly reduced. (This benefit alone may raise profit margins by 10% or more.) Beyond these savings are those realized in the improved business prospects for companies with a reputation for providing timely, high-quality products.

When CAD/CAM Is the Only Approach

Yet another measure of the value of CAD/CAM is the number of things it permits a company to do that could not be done before. These additional capabilities may be the difference between receiving a job contract and being passed over. As an example, numerical control (NC) applications allow the designer to create highly accurate tool paths. More efficient use of expensive NC machines translates into lower costs that can be passed on to the client. Another example is the automatic scaling function built into most CAD/CAM systems. Operators can use it to work on very large and very small constructions simultaneously, permitting engineering drawings that would be impossible to create manually. By offering more, a company can reasonably expect to generate more business for itself.

Three-Dimensional Designs

Too much cannot be said about the advantages of creating 3-dimensional rather than 2-dimensional designs. Visually, designers are at an enormous advantage when they are able to evaluate 3-dimensional designs. The ambiguity of 2-dimensional projections is no longer an issue. Three dimensions permit objects to be displayed in an infinite number of different views. Three-dimensional views imply much more complete data regarding a design than do 2-dimensional views. This fact alone results in more complete analysis than is possible when working in only 2 dimensions. Three-dimensional solids, to take the argument one step further, are complete and unambiguous models of the part, and can form the basis for a whole set of automated applications. Design time is reduced, design quality is increased. Savings can be enormous.

Evaluating These Benefits

What are we to make of these benefits? How can they be translated into dollar terms?

Arriving at some answers may take a little work, but the figures can open the eyes of even the most parsimonious executive. The only trick is to be as specific as possible.

Productivity ratios are determined by comparing costs against productivity benefits. The costs of implementing a CAD/CAM system can be divided into nonrecurring and recurring. Nonrecurring costs include the following:

1. Consulting fees (optional), including cost of feasibility studies and proposals
2. Price of system components
3. Shipping costs
4. Initial training fees
5. Cost of time lost during installation
6. Sales taxes
7. Facilities costs (air-conditioning installation, carpeting, room expansions, etc.)
8. Cost of creating an initial database

Each of these costs must be determined and listed individually.

The recurring costs include the following categories:

1. Maintenance and upgrade expenses
2. Supplies (paper, magnetic tape, etc.)
3. Downtime
4. Property taxes
5. Overhead (electricity, heating, floor space, etc.)
6. Ongoing training programs
7. Insurance
8. System improvements

These costs also must be listed individually and added to the total system expenses. Only by adding together both recurring and non-recurring costs can an accurate and believable evaluation be made of returns on investment. This, in turn, determines whether the system can be cost justified.

The other side of the coin is productivity improvement. This can be figured in a couple of different ways. The first is simply by comparing the number of hours required to complete a task before CAD/CAM implementation and after. The second is by comparing the amount of work that is done during a day or week or month before CAD/CAM and after.

The difficulty in the first method is that it often ends up lumping together jobs that are not automated by CAD/CAM along with jobs that are. This succeeds in watering down the productivity ratios and making them appear less significant than they really are. For example, in a shop with 20 people, they represent about 4,000 hours of labor per month. Suppose that only half that time is dedicated to manual drafting. If a CAD/CAM system reduces that 2,000 hours by a factor of 4, resulting in 500 hours of drafting, it still reduces the overall workload of the shop by only 1,500 hours. The resulting shop-wide productivity increase figures to be less than 2 to one, which is much below what we have come to expect from CAD/CAM.

Figured according to the total amount of drafting work being done, however, the equation reveals a much more substantial productivity ratio. Drafters can do in 500 hours what it took them 2000 hours to do before CAD/CAM. Four times as much work can be done in the same number of hours. These latter figures are much more realistic and are more exemplary of true productivity ratios.

Evaluating Customer Support Services

All CAD/CAM systems will break down. While 100% uptime may be the goal system vendors say they are working toward, it is unlikely they will ever achieve it. This makes customer support as much a factor in overall system performance as the hardware or software. Moreover, support is expensive (often equivalent to 25% of the initial system cost per year). Evaluating these services is an important part of system evaluation.

Typically, support falls into 2 categories: maintenance and upgrades. Maintenance fixes hardware and software problems. Upgrades enhance processing capacity by adding to or replacing components on an existing system. Both elements of system support directly affect productivity. Both should be defined in the sales contract.

Service response times and repair guarantees can be negotiated. The basis of these negotiations needs to be defined. Often the determination of whether the contract is being lived up to derives from a definition of downtime. It makes a considerable difference whether downtime is defined as a complete system failure or the failure of any single component such as a workstation or peripheral device. It should be spelled out in the contract.

As a point of interest, many vendors, for a premium, will write uptime guarantees into the contract. A common figure used with such guarantees is 98% uptime. When making these contracts the crucial determination is comparing the cost of downtime per hour with the costs of guaranteed uptime. It is not always to the customer's benefit to enter into such an agreement when the price is too high.

Another option is third-party service contracts. These are not highly recommended. Third-party service organizations often have limited access to spare parts and fewer field offices. Repair times are often twice as long as vendor repairs. The only advantage is lower price.

When evaluating a service organization, refer to the following questions:

1. Where is the nearest service office?
2. Is service available 24 hours a day?

3. How many people work at the nearest service office?
4. What are the escalation procedures in the event the service technician cannot fix the problem?
5. Where is the nearest parts depot?
6. Where is the nearest regional or district office?
7. What qualifications do the field service people have?
8. How many customers are supported by the field office?
9. How are service people dispatched?
10. Are remote diagnostics available?

When evaluating upgrade support a different set of questions must be asked:

1. How often are upgrades scheduled?
2. How often are they installed?
3. Do upgrades require the system to be out of service? If so, how long?
4. Are the upgrades dependable?
5. Do the upgrades address performance issues as well as processing needs?
6. Do the upgrades add enhancements at the expense of system performance?
6. How many people are assigned to do work on upgrades?
7. What are their qualifications?
8. Can upgrades be installed through remote telecommunications hook-ups?

The willingness and skill with which vendors deal with software deficiencies is the single most important indication of a company's dedication to upgrades. Software upgrades are expensive and difficult and if a company makes good on its promises to upgrade software, chances are hardware upgrades promises are good as well.

System Evaluation

The evaluation of any CAD/CAM system must be conducted against some established standard based on the purpose of the system. Why is the system being purchased and what is it expected to do? Only after defining this goal is a thorough evaluation possible.

Perhaps the most direct way of evaluating system performance is to design an evaluation form listing all important hardware and software components of the system. A point system can then be devised to rank each component according to some arbitrary scale, say, from one to 10, where one is unsatisfactory and 10 is superior. Each of the components is then assigned another number corresponding to its relative importance to the overall system. For instance, a system used primarily for drafting would have a high rating for graphics software and for plotting but a low rating for tool path generation and language capabilities. These ratings can also be assigned numbers according to an arbitrary scale of one to 10. By multiplying each performance rating by each importance rating a reasonably accurate profile can be obtained of overall system performance.

This method can be used effectively both before and after system purchase. When used before purchase, the results can help compare competing systems and evaluate benchmark performances. When used after system purchase, it can reveal how well the system has lived up to expectations and where the system might be upgraded or otherwise improved.

References

1. Joel Orr, "CAD and CAM Far from Being Integrated," *Computer Graphics Today* 1 (3) (September 1984).

2. Robert J. Stevenson and Terry Swanson, "LAN Extends CAD/CAM Capabilities," *Design News* 39 (5) (March 14, 1983): 208.

Additional Reading

Chasen, S.H. and Dow, J.W. *The Guide for the Evaluation and Implementation of CAD/CAM Systems,* CAD/CAM Decisions, Atlanta, GA, 1979.

Knox, Charles S. *CAD/CAM Systems: Planning and Implementation,* New York: Marcel Dekker, Inc., 1983.

Machine Design 56 (25) (November 8, 1984). This entire issue is dedicated to a discussion of CAD/CAM systems.

Chapter 8
System Management

This chapter pulls together all the major ideas developed in previous chapters and applies this background to the specific task of managing a CAD/CAM system from initial justification phases through final evaluation. It offers a comprehensive approach to CAD/CAM system management.

Management tasks have been divided into 4 separate but related areas: preparation, implementation, maintenance, and evaluation. Together this information implies a practical, useful, uniform approach to CAD/CAM system management.

The Evolution of CAD/CAM System Management

Techniques in computer system management have undergone enormous changes in the 40 years since computer technology was introduced to industry. These changes are due in part, of course, to the improvement in and refinement of management techniques themselves. But they are also largely due to the technological changes reflected in the computer systems that are in current use.

The earliest computer graphics installations, for example, which by now date back more than 30 years, were very expensive, highly centralized systems dependent upon a mainframe host computer. These computers were often at the center of a single data processing complex that conducted not only computer graphics functions but all other computerized information services for the company. As a result, only the very large and very profitable companies could afford the luxury of a computer graphics installation.

The situation has changed greatly in just the last 10 years. Computer graphics systems have become less expensive and less centralized. As we have seen, today many engineers have their own graphics systems running on standard electrical outlets in their own offices, and companies are spending less for those systems than they might spend on a large copy machine. The result is that many more companies are finding computer graphics systems viable solutions to their CAD/CAM processing problems.

As a direct consequence of these technological changes modern computer graphics departments no longer need be made up of a small group of professional scientists working under the management umbrella of a data processing manager. They now can be independently managed groups of skilled workers reporting directly to the engineering, design, or drafting departments of an organization. In other words, given the specialization of computer graphics and the independence such systems now have from mainframe hardware, the requirements for managing graphics systems are much different from those encountered in the past.

Nevertheless, just because management requirements are changing, this should not be taken to imply that computer graphics system management is any easier or any less important to the operation of that system. The acquisition and implementation of a computer graphics installation, precisely because of the degree of specialization built in to these new systems, still requires very careful and strategic management decisions. In some ways, the management skills required are more demanding than ever. There are more decisions to be made. Moreover, as we will see, those decisions must come from several levels within the company, including both executive management and technical management.

System Management Issues

The issues in computer graphics system management can be reduced to 4 separate but related tasks: (1) justifying the system; (2) implementing the system; (3) maintaining the system; and (4) evaluating the system. Management must prepare for these tasks thoroughly. No company can expect to manage a CAD/CAM facility efficiently by simply imposing existing management techniques on the computer graphics installation. Computer graphics systems represent, for most people, an entirely new technology and a new way of thinking about graphics production. The acquisition and management of the system must evolve together. This is singularly important. Therefore, it is imperative that all levels of management be involved in the justification and implementation of a graphics systems as well as in the long term maintenance and evaluation of the system.

Make no mistake, the installation of a computer graphics system, despite its being proven and accepted technology, will result in a tremendous upheaval within the engineering, design, and drafting organization of any company. Such dramatic changes do not come without some difficulty. The transition will always be smoother if it is well planned and if all employees are prepared.

Justifying the System

Justifying a computer graphics system is not as difficult as it once was because the technology by now is well established and is already touted in many industries as beneficial to design, drafting, and engineering processes. That much can be assumed. But more than just the technology must be justified before top management is likely to accept the idea. The system must also be justified as a capital expense and in terms of its specific applicability to the business of the company.

This justification is very important because no computer graphics installation is likely to succeed without the support of top management. In fact, management support is the most important element in the success of such a venture. Without support from the top, a computer graphics system may not be given enough time to prove its value and it may not receive the funds required to upgrade and expand as the technology improves. Without these advantages, even the best CAD/CAM installation will fail.

By and large then, the success of any data processing installation is dependent much more on the skill and support of the people involved than on the computer hardware and software. The system itself must be sound—no one would argue otherwise—but it is the people that make the system useful and effective. It is important, therefore, to prepare carefully for the implementation of a computer graphics system, because once the management and technical staff is in place and their modes of operation are established, it is very difficult to change them. This is particularly true of large installations at large corporations where bureaucracies can be formidable.

Getting Started

Companies getting started in computer graphics must first find someone to investigate the possibilities available to them. This person might be assigned the task by senior management based on merit and aptitude, or might be the person whose previous interest in computer graphics first brings the possibilities of this new technology to the attention of senior management, or might be a hired outside consultant. In any case, senior management should lend authority to the investigation, thus enabling the person to pursue the subject thoroughly. Armed with both responsibility and authority, the investigator should be allowed, indeed encouraged, to attend computer graphics trade shows and seminars, to contact industry consultants and other computer graphics specialists, and to visit existing computer graphics installations. These kinds of firsthand experiences with existing computer graphics installations and with working graphics system operators and managers are especially important, because relatively little reliable literature yet exists on the subject, and because the technology is developing and changing with such rapidity. There is no other way to be sure that the information being compiled is both complete and up-to-date.

With the basic background information gathered, the next step is to decide exactly what applications the company wants to address with computer graphics technology. This determination is the single most important part of the justification phase for computer graphics because it determines how, where, and to what extent computer graphics will be integrated into the working procedures of the company.

All aspects of the company's business that are to be, or could be converted from manual to computer graphics procedures must be pinpointed and defined. This means that all departments within the company must be surveyed to determine what possible applications could be required of the computer graphics system. This ensures that both immediate and long-term needs in CAD/CAM are accounted for. The findings of this survey are reviewed in light of the information compiled by the outside research and become the basis for determining the configuration of the system that is finally implemented and for suggesting long-term plans and goals for possible expansion of the installation in the future.

As an important adjunct to these findings some determination must be made about the order in which required computing tasks need to be done and the volume of each of those tasks. A set of priorities can then be developed to determine which department(s) should have their systems installed first. Once this information is compiled and well understood throughout the company, the step-by-step changeover to computer graphics will be better accepted and more orderly than if done without such a plan.

The Proposal

Once the information is gathered on the types of CAD/CAM systems available and on the specific requirements of the system, it is time to evaluate the findings and to determine whether CAD/CAM is a feasible solution to the company's design and drafting needs. This determination should be based on studies of cost-effectiveness, available capital, and the existing labor force. If a CAD/CAM system approach to design or production tasks is determined feasible, the information can be presented to management as a formal proposal.

Selling management on the idea of computer graphics and on the viability of CAD/CAM systems is essential. The installation of a computer graphics system is more than just another capital investment. It is an innovation that will affect the total operation of a company from product design through production. The impact of CAD/CAM on a company is significant enough to demand active involvement by top management. Therefore, the proposal should instill a belief in management of the long-term benefits of computer graphics technology.

The proposal must contain a clear and concise justification of computer graphics technology itself. One way of doing this is by describing the product design cycle and pointing out the benefits that can be realized along each step of the way when a computer graphics system is involved.

Consider for a moment how a product design develops. First, a need is perceived. Second, the goal of fulfilling that need is adopted. Third, the goal is broken down into its constituent tasks and each is delineated as specifically as possible. Fourth, a design idea is formed which satisfies the requirements of the specifications. Fifth, the design is analyzed and refined. Sixth, the whole process is repeated, the ideas refined, until the design problem is solved.

This is a very abstract process. It takes place largely in the designer's head. Yet the ideas being worked are generally visual. How often have we heard the phrase "I am having difficulty visualizing what is at issue here," or, more simply, "This problem is hard to visualize." Computer graphics technology is a perfect tool to facilitate such visualization. In that alone, such a system can reduce design time. It allows the designers to see what they are thinking, to visualize abstract ideas in a way that allows them to refine their thinking at each step. When that is coupled with the analytical ability a CAD/CAM system can bring to bear on the model, the designer is made more efficient than he or she could ever be when using manual design methods.

Yet there is much more at issue than efficiency in the design and drafting departments. There are significant consequences to this faster design cycle. Management must be prepared to act much more rapidly than before on product development decisions. The production staff must be prepared to receive product specifications faster, more often, and in greater detail. The marketing staff must be prepared to provide faster support for new products and faster input to management on these new products and on the relative positions of competitors who may also be using computer graphics techniques. These are important points for top management to understand as they go about the task of deciding whether or not to purchase computer graphics equipment and they should be dealt with clearly in the proposal.

Other more technical information is important to the proposal as well. For instance, the proposal should include a variety of ancillary information on site planning, personnel, training, and data output requirements. This information should be made as specific as possible. The proposal should also contain some general price guidelines upon which the final decision can be based.

Implementing the System

The next step, assuming top management has given its support, is to begin to implement the computer graphics installation. The graphics system requirements are by now clearly outlined and agreed upon. These requirements must now be matched with a system configuration. A number of possibilities exist, including all of the following:

1. A dedicated turnkey graphics system with host minicomputer
2. One or more graphics workstations linked to a host
3. One or more stand-alone graphics workstations
4. A time sharing configuration with an existing mainframe
5. A local area network of stand-alone graphics workstations
6. A custom built system designed to meet unique company specifications
7. A service bureau
8. Some combination of the above

A committee consisting of one member of each department interested in acquiring computer graphics capabilities should study the system configuration question carefully. The decision should be made not only with regard for the current processing needs but with attention paid to anticipated processing needs as they develop in the future. The upgradeability of a computer graphics system is very important given the astonishing rapidity with which the technology is evolving.

It is quite possible that more than one configuration from more than one CAD/CAM vendor will fulfill the requirements for computer graphics set out in the proposal. If this turns out to be true, several management issues should be considered during the discussions to help distinguish competing systems. For example, managing a turnkey CAD/CAM system with, say, 8 dependent workstations is quite a different proposition from managing 8 stand-alone graphics workstations or 8 stand-alone workstations in a local area network.

In the first case, the hardware dependency of the workstations require them to be in close proximity with one another. In such a configuration they can be easily monitored and controlled by a single system manager with access to the central processor and main disk storage units. In the latter cases, the individual workstations are largely independent of one another and, in fact, may be located miles apart; there is no unified system, as such, to manage. The system manager might well be replaced by a department manager who is responsible for overseeing production work rather than the allocation of hardware or software resources. In other words, a centralized computer graphics system implies centralized management of that system, whereas decentralized systems imply decentralized management. The politics of these options should not be ignored.

In general, there are 2 ways to go when assigning management responsibility for the CAD/CAM installation. Either it can be managed as part of a larger data processing group, or it can be managed as a separate CAD/CAM department. There are several good reasons for preferring the latter course.

One reason is cost. Mini- or microprocessor-based CAD/CAM systems can be brought on-line faster than mainframe data processing (DP) systems and can become productive sooner. They also allow the engineering and manufacturing departments to bypass the several additional layers of management that always seem to control company-wide management information systems (MIS). Dedicated CAD/CAM systems also eliminate complex interdepartmental accounting considerations, thus further lowering operating overhead.

A second reason is that CAD/CAM systems are used for engineering and manufacturing tasks that are quite alien to those hired to run generalized data processing systems. Only the engineering, design, and production staffs are likely to know how to perform and evaluate CAD/CAM processing. Data processing people will have a hard time managing resources they do not fully understand. This situation is exacerbated by CAD/CAM vendors who direct their marketing efforts at the engineering and manufacturing staffs that their products are designed to service. This tends to alienate further the MIS/DP staff from the CAD/CAM installation.

Personnel

Personnel may influence which computer graphics system is chosen. The people who will spend the most time actually working with the system are likely to be engineers, designers, drafters, illustrators, and architects, not people whose primary background is computers or computer graphics. Their knowledge will pertain more directly to the *application* of the computer graphics system than to the system itself. Therefore, in a situation where no systems analyst is available, the application software must match closely the needs of the operators. In situations where custom software is required or where modifications to the system are anticipated after installation, someone with a computer science background may have to be hired.

In making these decisions it is always best, for several reasons, to try to use personnel already with the company. For one, the organization of a computer graphics installation is dependent on a knowledge of how a particular company conducts its research, design, and drafting functions. The configuration of the system should fit the established working and organizational patterns of the company. This makes for a more orderly transition period. For another, designers, drafters, engineers, et al, usually relish the idea of having access to new technology that will make their jobs more interesting. A CAD/CAM installation, if implemented correctly, can have a very positive effect on company morale. In fact, as the system is being fully implemented, management should take care not to allow expectations to grow beyond reasonable limits. The implementation of a computer graphics system is better viewed as an evolutionary process than a revolutionary one, and expectations should be formed accordingly.

Training. User expectations will become more realistic as familiarity with the system grows. Virtually all CAD/CAM system vendors provide customer training classes. They can provide a valuable introduction to computer graphics technology for personnel who are soon to be using that technology. The classes lessen the frustration and anxiety of facing a computer system for the first time. All the system users should be encouraged to enroll in these classes before the new system is actually delivered on-site. It will prepare them to pick up with their work immediately after the system is installed.

Accepting Bids

With a system configuration and description defined it is time to begin accepting bids from CAD/CAM system vendors. The price of equipment will, of course, be a major determining factor in which vendor receives the contract. But another valuable method of evaluating comparable systems is by conducting a benchmark test. By comparing the time it takes different vendors to do the same job, and by comparing the output from that job, the advantages and disadvantages of various systems become more clear. If a benchmark task is representative of the work that will regularly be done by the system, the benchmark may be a very accurate gauge of the suitability of that system in meeting the given computer graphics requirements set out in the proposal.

A request for bids is often made by releasing a document called the "request for proposal" (RFP). This document is a public invitation for all qualified CAD/CAM vendors to submit information describing how their products will satisfy the processing requirements of the customer. It is important, therefore, that the RFP contain an accurate and complete description of the design and manufacturing tasks the customer expects to address within the impending CAD/CAM system. (For more information on how to organize and draft an RFP, refer to Appendix II.)

When at last a successful bidder is determined and the equipment has been ordered, a number of things occur rather rapidly. The physical facilities must be prepared. Most vendors have their own experts who help with this process and provide input prior to the time the contract is actually signed. The organizational moves, if any, should be made so that the mechanisms for managing the facility are in place by the time the equipment arrives. In addition, work procedures and data base issues should be explored so that work can commence in an orderly fashion as soon as the equipment is operational.

The acceptance test is the final part of system implementation. The specifications for this test are usually spelled out in the sales agreement beforehand, and payment is contingent upon the system passing the test in all its aspects. The test is conducted after the system is installed. It is simply a rundown of all the standard modes of operation to ensure that the hardware and software are fully operational.

All of these implementation procedures must be conducted with care because they will determine, to a very large degree, how successfully the system can be maintained. If standard operating procedures set up during the implementation phase turn out to be unworkable, a great deal of time and data will be lost trying to rectify the situation. It is better to prepare early for an orderly and logical transition than to end up with a system that is a technological or managerial deadend.

Maintaining the System

Most system maintenance is routine. It is part of the standard, daily operating procedures of a computer graphics installation. General guidelines as well as required preventive maintenance tasks are outlined in the technical documentation accompanying all computer graphics systems. Systems managers should take the time to read this material carefully.

Preventive Maintenance

Preventive maintenance includes such things as keeping the working areas clean and free from magnetic interference, maintaining temperature and humidity levels within acceptable ranges, lubricating or dusting moving parts, and running canned diagnostic checks on the electronics. Much of this work is done by the field engineer assigned to the installation by the vendor as part of the standard maintenance contract.

System Maintenance

Other kinds of system maintenance must be managed by someone within the company. Typically these tasks fall into one of 5 categories: (1) managing system output; (2) managing system input; (3) managing the data base; (4) managing system security; and (5) presenting system management decisions to users. Usually all of these tasks are assigned to the system manager. The tasks require a knowledge of the technology involved in addition to some aptitude for managing people. Very often the system manager has a background in computer science and system analysis.

System Output

A great deal of information regarding the requirements for data output is compiled during the system justification and implementation phases of system management. This information needs to be applied to the methods of data output made available by the computer graphics system. The system manager must review the output requirements, define the contents of output reports, determine what output media are available and appropriate in each case, and consider how the output is to be disseminated and stored.

System Input

The method by which users input data, despite being determined largely by the equipment and software available to each user, requires management decisions. For instance, once output requirements are decided upon, it may become clear that a certain kind of input not previously considered is now, in fact, required due to a change in the output implications of a certain kind of report. Such determinations will dictate not only *how* some data are entered, but *whether* they are entered.

Other system input decisions must also be made, such as determining what media will be used to store on-line data and how input files will be grouped. The system manager must also be concerned with the format of reports and the amount of disk space available and how it should be allotted in order to accomodate data. These decisions must be made with some care because they determine how efficiently the system is used and whether the input data are stored in a useful form.

System Data Base

Managing the system data base is perhaps the most difficult and time-consuming task of the system manager. The most important aspect of this task is determining exactly what information must be in the data base. This determination should be made in consultation with all the users of the CAD/CAM system, thus assuring them the information they need to conduct their work is present and accessible.

In addition, the system manager ascertains how data files should be stored in relation to one another. That is, he or she must decide how files must be arranged within a logical hierarchy (such as libraries or directories) so that users can find related information easily. A set of system controls must also be instituted to ensure that data are input accurately and not corrupted. These controls include regulating file-naming conventions, establishing guidelines for numbering and dating reports, and maintaining and updating often-used programs.

Also among the data base management duties is the imposition of some kind of data back-up procedures. All new data must be copied off-line for safekeeping as archives and to prevent missing data in the event of system failures or other catastrophic system or user errors. In this way valuable data can be restored on-line after the error is diagnosed and rectified. Back-ups should be conducted regularly on all computer graphics systems.

System Security

Related to the task of data base management is the more general issue of system security. System security measures are built into nearly all computer graphics systems and should be integrated intelligently into daily processing activities. These measures prevent users from corrupting one another's data and permit only authorized users to have access to the system. Specific methods for maintaining system security are outlined in the technical documentation accompanying each system. Typically they include such measures as requiring special passwords to log on to the system and having several types of user accounts, each with a different set of priorities and access codes.

Presentation to Users

No management decisions concerning the use of the CAD/CAM system will be effective without the understanding and cooperation of the system users. All of the system management issues should be openly discussed with the operating personnel. There is no benefit in keeping system management secrets from the day-to-day users of the system. System efficiency and durability depends on the willingness of operators to abide by simple rules of data processing conduct. Periodic seminars involving the system manager and all system users provide a valuable forum for making these issues known.

Evaluating the System

After the computer graphics system has been successfully installed and is fully integrated into the business activities of the company, it should be subjected to periodic evaluation. The purpose of this evaluation is twofold: first, to determine whether the system is being used to best advantage; and second, to determine whether the system should be upgraded or otherwise improved. The following sections take up issues that should be a part of any system evaluation.

Ease of Use

A modern computer graphics system should be easy to use. Not only should the interactive software be accessible even to novice users, but the equipment itself should be comfortable and convenient to use in a standard business office environment. Moreover, the system should be flexible enough to accomodate a variety of operators each employing individual working habits.

Data Base Intelligence

The computer graphics data base might best be viewed as a reservoir of knowledge related to the specific application for which the graphics system is being used. Greater knowledge translates into better results. Therefore, as the data base grows, the work being done with the system should become easier and better with each project. The data base should be able to associate and analyze related data and should provide all the properties a user needs to assign to data—such as part numbers, color, three-dimensionality, solidity, etc.

Software Dependability

No software system is without errors. Nevertheless, errors cannot be tolerated within critical routines or in situations that result in system failures. Habitual fatal errors in graphics system software are unacceptable and should be reported to the system vendor. A graphics system software component that is fully operational less than 96% of the time is unreliable and should be returned to the vendor for additional debugging.

Software Functionality. Operators must be provided with adequate tools. The most important tools in a graphics system are software dependent. These include not only basic graphics functions but system management tools as well (such as back-up and system security utilities). Any inadequacies should be reported to the system vendor in the form of software improvement requests.

Documentation

A computer graphics system is only as good as its technical documentation. These documents are the primary reference source for all system users. Users should expect their operating manuals to be accurate and complete. If this expectation is not met, complaints to the vendor should be loud and long.

Upgradeability. As the volume of work done on a computer graphics system grows, management may want to consider how the system can be improved or expanded. The ease with which upgrades can be instituted should be an important consideration when installing a computer graphics system. New graphics system components are only useful when they can be integrated quickly and easily into the existing system.

Overall System Dependability

The system manager is responsible for keeping track of system downtime. This information should be reviewed and charted to give management an idea of the percent of working time during which the system is running normally. No system can be expected to run all the time, but system uptime can reasonably be expected to stay between 96% and 98%.

Quality of Technical Support

The speed with which field engineering support personnel respond to system problems and the quality of that support often determine the overall dependability of any computer system. Users should be able to depend on the vendor's support staff not only to fix immediate problems but to advise them on standard operating procedures, on preventive maintenance, and on the advisability and availability of system hardware and software upgrades. It is a good idea to keep a record of all service calls, including the reason for the call, how long it took for the field engineer to respond, how long the system was down, and whether a similar problem had ever occurred before.

Production Levels

A properly installed CAD/CAM system can always increase production levels. If production levels are not improving gradually in accordance with the users' familiarity with the system, a wholesale evaluation of the company's computer graphics requirements is in order.

General User Satisfaction

Computer graphics systems are intended to make the job easier for engineers, designers, drafters, illustrators, and all other users. If users are not satisfied that the system is enhancing their ability to accomplish their job, something needs to be changed. User satisfaction is the most important criterion in evaluating the efficacy of a computer graphics installation.

Additional Reading

Hall, R.H. *Organizations: Structure and Process.* 2d ed. Englewood Cliffs, NJ: Prentice-Hall, 1977.

Miles, R.E. and Snow, C.C. *Organizational Strategy, Structure, and Process.* New York: McGraw Hill, Inc., 1978.

Newman, William and Sproull, Robert. *Principles of Interactive Computer Graphics.* 2d ed. New York: McGraw Hill, Inc., 197?.

Shelly, Gary B. and Cashman, Thomas J. *Introduction to Computers and Data Processing.* Brea, CA: Anaheim Publishing Co. 1980.

Siders, R.A. et al. *Computer Graphics: A Revolution in Design.* New York: American Management Association, 1966.

Szilagyi, Andrew D., Jr. and Wallace, Marc J. *Organizational Behavior and Performance.* 3d ed. Glenview, IL: Scott, Foresman and Co., 1983.

Appendix I
The Use of Color

Color displays are relatively new to the graphics industry. Only in the last 3 to 4 years have color display graphics workstations become the norm and not the exception, which has brought about a new attitude toward using color. No longer is it regarded an extravagance. Today most CAD/CAM operators would consider themselves handicapped without it.

In contrast with years past, more than 75% of all the workstations now sold are equipped with color displays. Why is this?

On the surface it would seem a difficult question to answer. Color display is substantially more expensive than black and white. Color is more difficult and more expensive to represent on hard copy media. Color displays cause eye fatigue more readily than monochrome. Color is another, major source of operator errors. Moreover, color can illicit unwanted emotional or stereotypic responses in viewers.

Nonetheless, color workstations are now the standard for computer graphics installations. For CAD/CAM vendors to remain competitive, they must continue to pursue technology that uses color—and they must do more. It is important that they understand why clients are so certain they need color workstations.

Color is an extraordinarily versatile tool. That is enough to explain its recent popularity. Just because it may also be fun or amusing is no reason to discount its importance to CAD/CAM workstation operators. After all, color has meaning. It can be used to integrate, emphasize, or obscure data. It can inform viewers. It can even be made to persuade and to influence opinion—as any advertiser or political campaign manager would be willing to attest. Since the technology is well-tested and readily available, it stands to reason that color should be added to the repertoire of common graphics tools.

Consider the benefits. Color enables engineers and draftsmen to represent both natural and manufactured objects more realistically, lending credibility to the displays. Color can be used to highlight particularly noteworthy data. It can identify similar parts within a displayed object using a color key. It can depict logical relations among those parts. Color can increase legibility in complex drawings, or it can enhance the visual appeal of a display giving it more impact.

As with any complex tool, there is a challenge in learning to use it well. The use of color has many pitfalls. For instance, most observers can only keep track of 10 or 12 colors when distinguishing patterns or color-coded information. Maps or charts employing too many hues will be more confusing than monochrome reproductions of the same data. As another example designers should be careful not to mask important information with a weak color or by using a color having no contrast against the background of a drawing. Engineers and draftsmen are now finding themselves in a position of learning what visual artists have always known: color is a very complex medium of communication.

This does not mean users should be discouraged from using it—quite the opposite. Color adds a new dimension to the creative process; it revitalizes routine jobs, encourages creativity, enhances a designer's sense of contruction and harmony and balance. Color ameliorates the whole design and drafting process. It may even help CAD/CAM operators approach their jobs with more energy and anticipation.

Computer graphics workstations should be expected to live up to their potential as tools that enable users to better visualize their design and manufacturing problems. One way of doing this is with color.

Following are suggestions for how color can best be used in visual display devices.[1]

1. Avoid the simultaneous display of spectrally extreme colors such as red and blue or yellow and purple. This helps reduce the need for continual refocusing which can result in eye fatigue.
2. Avoid using pure blue for the display of text, thin lines, or small shapes. The physiology of the human eye makes it difficult to focus on blue, which therefore makes blue very appropriate for background color.

3. Avoid using reds or greens in the periphery of large-scale displays. The periphery of the human eye is insensitive to these colors. Yellows and blues are much better peripheral colors.
4. Opponent colors go well together and are good for simple color displays. Red and green or yellow and blue make good combinations.
5. Avoid single-color distinctions. People with any degree of color blindness may have trouble distinguishing colors that are not mixed. Use a variety of colors in a display wherever possible. An interesting footnote is that color deficient observers may have more trouble distinguishing elements in a monochromatic display than in a color display because of a diminished ability to discern brightness levels on monochromatic screens.
6. Use brightness as well as color to help observers see edges and boundaries in displayed images. It is difficult to focus on edges created by color alone.
7. Be aware that colors change in appearance as the level of ambient light changes. Displayed images should be colored with attention to whether they will be viewed in natural light or under florescent or incandescent lights.

Reference

1. These guidelines were adapted from "Physiological Principles for the Effective Use of Color," by Gerald Murch, *IEEE Computer Graphics and Applications* 4 (11) (November 1984): 49-54.

Additional Reading

Albers, J. *Interaction of Color*. New Haven, CT: Yale University Press, 1975.

Krebs, K.L. and Judd, D.B. "Design Principles for the Use of Color in Displays." *Proceedings of the Society for Information Display* 20 (First Quarter 1979): 10-15.

Truckenbrod, J. "Effective Use of Color in Computer Graphics." *Computer Graphics* 15 (August 1981): 83-90.

Appendix II
The Request for Proposal (RFP)

When a customer has decided to buy CAD/CAM technology, formulation of the Request For Proposal (RFP) is the last important, preparatory step before receiving bids from CAD/CAM vendors. The RFP uses information gathered during feasibility studies, costs analyses, and business planning to set out, in very specific terms, the requirements that must be fulfilled by the CAD/CAM system finally purchased by that company. Those requirements include performance characteristics, pricing constraints, maintenance agreements, and technical specifications.

This one document, to a very large degree, determines the CAD/CAM system that is finally installed. It is especially important for large contracts, where a great deal of money rides on the outcome of competitive bidding. RFPs are standard operating procedure for government contracts and in many other large businesses.

The purpose of the request for proposal is to solicit proposals from CAD/CAM vendors on how they would address the technology needs of the requesting company. With these proposals in hand, the company can better judge which of the contending systems is best suited to their processing needs.

A well-constructed RFP will result in very revealing responses. The document should be written with care—preferably by a professional.

What Does an RFP Contain?

A properly constructed RFP is much more than a list of technical specifications that must be satisfied. Those specifications only make sense when they follow a comprehensive set of bidding instructions and a description of any other special or unique conditions that may apply.

An RFP is a formal, public document, and it is customary to introduce it with a cover letter inviting each vendor to bid on the contract. This is not a form letter but is addressed to each vendor separately, inviting their participation in the proposal process. The letter should list all those vendors invited to participate, thereby notifying each vendor of the competitive nature of the request.

Following the letter is a list of instructions, conditions, or special terms that must be followed when submitting a bid. These include such easily overlooked bits of information as the deadline for the proposal and the address to which it must be sent, explanations of state and federal licensing and tax obligations, confidentiality guidelines, and delivery date requirements.

Also included in the RFP is a list of special information such as financial data, e.g., 10-K Securities and Exchange Commission reports, a list of executive officers, pricing schedules, and site inspection requirements. This information must be clear and unequivocal; companies wanting to do it right will hire or assign a professional writer to produce the final draft.

Most RFPs also require a benchmark, and a document should be included which describes this process. The benchmark demands should be reasonable, but not too lenient. Ideally, a benchmark is a comparison test of competing systems that illustrates how each system would perform under conditions resembling a normal production environment. (See Chapter 5.) Specific guidelines for the benchmark will discourage proposals from patently unqualified vendors and encourage proposals from vendors particularly suited to the task. On the other hand, if the RFP does not require a benchmark test, this also should be stated.

Technical Specifications

The bulk of the RFP addresses technical specifications. This section constitutes a complete description of the system's functional requirements. This does not mean, however, that the RFP sets out a hard and fast description of the exact system configuration. Each vendor should be left free to recommend a product or set of products which fulfills the functional requirements.

The technical specifications section can be organized in several ways and each customer will doubtless do it a little differently. Nonetheless, it is clear what topics must be considered.

First of all, it is important to describe the purpose of the system. ·This statement then becomes the yardstick used to measure the extent to which each proposal satisfies the technical requirements. The statement, therefore, must be specific and include a description of every kind of processing required of the CAD/CAM system. It should also make some comment on which departments will be using the system and how each department is expected to be managed. A good conclusion to this statement might be a brief description of the reasons for pursuing the CAD/CAM alternative to current production methods.

The real meat of the RFP follows: descriptions of the hardware and software requirements. When drawing up the software requirements it is important not only to include a list of the graphics system and applications software, but the operating system requirements as well. The reasons for this are described in more detail in Chapter 5, but they can be distilled down to the observation that the operating system generally controls all system security and data management functions.

In this section of the document, some mention also should be made of the software interface and communications requirements. Without these requirements clearly spelled out, the customer may end up with a totally isolated system incapable of being upgraded with hardware or software bought from any other but the original vendor. In these days of CAD/CAM specialization, it is advisable not to be locked in to one vendor. No single vendor can possibly provide all the solutions a given customer may need, but they can be expected to provide sufficient interfaces and standard data formats enabling the customer to find and employ processing solutions from other sources.

The hardware requirements can be somewhat less stringent. Many different workstation designs, for instance, may be adequate to fulfill the needs of the system. It is sufficient to list guidelines for the number of workstations, the processing speed, ergonomic requirements, and categories of output devices, rather than to list specific models and configurations for this hardware. Data storage requirements are the exception to this rule, and can be spelled out more precisely, e.g., the exact size of the disks or the read/write density of the magnetic tape drives.

Support Requirements

Following the technical requirements section (some people may choose to make it part of the technical requirements) is a description of the customer support and maintenance issues that proposals are required to address. Some of these descriptions ought to be very specific. For instance, vendors should be required to respond to customer service calls with on-site support within 24 hours. It is advisable to have such a stipulation written directly into the sale contract when the time comes.

Other support requirements need to be spelled out in similar detail. Preventive maintenance should not be allowed to interfere with normal daily processing tasks, but should be done during off-hours or in such a way as not to impair system operation in any way. Software upgrades must be made available by the vendor on a regular schedule. A provision should be made for producing software patches between major upgrades to resolve major system bugs. And in all of these things, there has to be some significant consequence when the vendor fails to live up to the terms of the agreement; otherwise, these support requirements are unenforcable and might as well be left out of the RFP.

Documentation

System documentation includes all user manuals, service manuals, operations manuals, and any printed reference cards that describe the software and hardware components of the system. These documents should be available for review when the proposal is submitted. Therefore, a request for copies of all manuals should be written into the RFP.

A much touchier subject is whether software source code should be submitted as part of the documentation. Most established vendors will steadfastly refuse to divulge source code, citing breach of security. New or smaller vendors can sometimes be persuaded to submit source code by the argument that the customer will be left without software support should the vendor go bankrupt or otherwise dissolve. When dealing with small or financially uncertain vendors, it is a good idea to include a provision in the

RFP for outright purchase of the software source code should the vendor go out of business.

Training

As described in Chapter 6, training is an important part of any CAD/CAM system and should be included in the RFP. Vendors must be asked to provide a complete description of their training courses and facilities, including a list of all training personnel and their backgrounds. Vendors not offering a comprehensive training program should be summarily rejected as candidates for receiving a CAD/CAM purchase order.

Acceptance Test

Provisions for an acceptance test ought to be written into the RFP. Do not assume that vendors will deliver equipment that is fully operational and up to technical specifications. *Put it in writing* that the customer is under no obligation to pay for equipment that does not operate to the terms of the contract. A definition of reasonable system failure should also be written into the contract to help determine what constitutes failure to comply with the acceptance agreement.

Summary

A good, general outline to follow when organizing an RFP includes:
1. Cover letter (invitation to bid)
2. Special instructions or conditions
3. List of other inclusions (financial forms, list of officers, etc.)
4. Benchmark demands
5. Technical specifications
   a. Purpose of the system
   b. List of departments involved
   c. Statement explaining why you are pursuing the CAD/CAM alternative

    d. Hardware requirements
    e. Software requirements
    f. Support requirements
    g. Documentation requirements
    h. Training requirements
    i. Acceptance test guidelines

When following this outline, it is important to keep in mind the purpose of an RFP. It is intended to reveal the CAD/CAM system vendor best suited to fulfilling the terms of the implied sales contract. Nothing is to be gained by producing an RFP that is unreasonably complex, obscure, or demanding. The language should be clear and straightforward, the organization simple and easy to follow. All important legal and financial matters need to be included, in addition to the technical specifications. Vendors should be given adequate time to respond thoroughly. Above all, the document should be complete; do not presume to leave out even the most obvious information.

Glossary

The following glossary includes many of the important computer graphics and CAD/CAM terms used in this book. It is by no means comprehensive to the computer graphics or CAD/CAM industries. Readers looking for a more complete glossary of such terms are advised to consult *The Computer Graphics Glossary,* (The Oryx Press, 1983).

Acceptance Test. A test evaluating the conformance of system hardware or software to predetermined specifications. This test is often specified in the sales contract between CAD/CAM system customers and vendors, and payment is contingent upon the system passing the test.

Access Time. The interval between the moment data are called from memory and the moment transmission is completed to the calling device. The interval is most often used when describing transmissions to a display device. Access time is commonly used as a means of comparing performance among CAD/CAM systems.

Addressable Point. Any position on a graphics system output device that can be specified by coordinates.

Aliasing. The visual effect that occurs on a display screen whenever the degree of detail in the displayed image exceeds the resolution available on the output device.

Analysis. The calculation of engineering or geometric properties by a CAD/CAM system. Specialized analysis programs are available from most CAD/CAM vendors as optional application software packages.

Application. A set of tasks that must be accomplished as part of a CAD/CAM enterprise. These tasks are addressed with a special set of programs, called application software, that are written specifically for the requirements of an application.

Benchmark. A reference point from which measurements can be made for comparison. CAD/CAM system customers commonly ask vendors to perform a test, consisting of some standard processing task, the results of which are used to compare the speed and accuracy of the systems before the purchase decision is made.

CAD/CAM (Computer-Aided Design/Computer-Aided Manufacturing). Refers to the application of computer technology to any or all aspects of the production process from design to fabrication.

Cathode-Ray Tube (CRT). A vacuum tube used for the display of on-line graphic data. It produces a visible pattern when its electron beam is focused on a small section of a luminescent screen. The beam can be varied in location and intensity to display any form.

Central Procesing Unit (CPU). That part of a computing system containing the circuits that control and execute all instructions that perform work on data in the system. These circuits include storage registers, arithmetic and logic units, and special register groups.

Clipping. Refers to any graphics data outside a specified boundary that are removed from the display or the file. It is most often used in mapping applications to remove data that would otherwise confuse the map being represented. Sometimes refers to the graphic data that are outside the viewing area of a drawing displayed on a cathode-ray tube.

Command-Driven. Describes a computer graphics system that operates only when a user enters specified key words followed by qualifying parameters. Contrast with "Menu-Driven."

Component. 1. Any set of graphic data that can be named and stored as an independent file. 2. In geometry, describes one of a set of 2 or more vectors having a sum equal to some other designated vector. 3. Any individual hardware or software part that is used to construct a turnkey CAD/CAM system.

Computer Graphics. Describes the use of computer technology to create or manipulate pictorial data of any kind.

Cutter Path. The line described by the motion of a cutting tool controlled by a CAD/CAM system. Also the graphic data representing that line in a graphics file.

Data Processing. Refers to any sequence of machine-controlled operations which act on data to produce some predictable, desired result. CAD/CAM is a subset of the data processing industry.

Digitizer. A peripheral device often associated with computer graphics systems that converts pictorial information into digital form. In a typical application, a drawing is placed on the surface of the device and is traced by the operator with a cursor or stylus. The traced form is then converted to digital data that can be processed by the central processing unit.

Dimension. 1. Noun: Any measure of spatial extent. 2. Verb: refers to the creation or determination of spatial extent for a given object.

Display Device. Any output device capable of producing a visual representation of graphic data. The most common display devices are cathode-ray tube screens, plotters, and hard copy units. Usually, however, the term refers to cathode-ray tubes.

Distributed Processing. Refers to the processing of data in a distributed computer network environment. This kind of processing permits data sharing and peripheral sharing by a group of separate computers with the effect of making more efficient use of resources than is usually possible in centralized processing.

Edit. Refers to the process of rearranging or modifying on-line data. In CAD/CAM, editing consists primarily of modifying the graphic data of drawings and figures.

Ergonomics. The study of the physical relationship between people and their work environment. The term is often applied more specifically to the study of fitting production equipment to the physical and behavioral characteristics of workers.

File. Any collection of logically related data. These data may then be stored, accessed, or otherwise processed as a single unit.

Function Keys. Refers to the input keys on data entry devices which, when pressed, initiate a particular processing operation on a CAD/CAM system. In this way, users can with a single keystroke activate functions that might otherwise require a long series of keystrokes to initiate.

Grid. Any pattern of horizontal and vertical lines that form squares of uniform size over a surface. In computer graphics, grids form the basis by which point positions are defined.

Hard Copy. A printed copy of graphic data produced on or stored by a computer graphics system.

Hidden Lines. Refers to those line segments of a graphic entity that would be obscured from view were the object displayed as a solid 3-dimensional figure.

Host Computer. The central processing unit which provides processing support to other processors, workstations, or peripheral devices. The devices being supported usually cannot function on their own, whereas the host can and does operate independently.

Interactivity. A data processing context in which the computer system and the user work together to solve problems. Usually the interactivity consists of the software prompting the user for information which is then processed in a predetermined way.

Layering. A logical concept that associates subgroups of graphic data within a single drawing. It allows the operator to view only those parts of a drawing being worked on and reduces the confusion that might result from viewing all parts of a very cluttered or complex file. Layers can conveniently be thought of as a series of transparencies that may be laid on top of one another in any order.

Menu-Driven. Describes a computer graphics system that operates when a user selects an option from a set of options displayed on the workstation screen. Contrast with "Command-Driven."

Networking. Refers to a special kind of system configuration in which 2 or more central processors are linked, enabling them to share work loads and data bases. Each processor participating in such a network is called a "node." It is sometimes used synonomously with "distributed processing."

Numerical Control (NC). Refers to the use of CAD/CAM systems to control and regulate manufacturing tools such as lathes, die cutters, metal bending equipment, flame cutters, etc.

Optical Scanner. A device that can view graphic images, sense the light emitted and, thereby, the position of the images, and translate those findings into on-line data comprehensible to a CAD/CAM system.

Peripheral Device. Any hardware component of a computing system distinct from the central processing unit but controlled by it for use in data input, output, or both.

Photocell. A photoelectric cell. A light-sensitive device which translates variations in light into corresponding variations in electrical signals. Used in light pens.

Pixel. The smallest unit available for display on a raster screen, representing a single graphics point. The word is derived from the term "picture element."

Potentiometer. An electromechanical device used to measure or to change the resistence in an electrical circuit. Used on CAD/CAM systems to operate input devices such as joysticks, roller balls, and touchpads.

Primitive. The most basic of graphic entities available on a graphics system including such items as points, line segments, characters, or geometric figures.

Prompt. Any message output by a computer system that requires some response from the operator. Systems that display prompts are said to be interactive.

Raster. Describes a type of cathode-ray tube in which a pattern of scanning lines divide the display area into addressable points. Raster display tubes are generally faster and less expensive that vector tubes and are, therefore, gaining popularity for use with CAD/CAM systems.

Resolution. 1. Refers to the ability of a graphics output device to make distinguishable the individual parts of an object or other images that are very close together in a drawing. 2. The smallest distance that can be processed accurately by a CAD/CAM system.

Stand-Alone. Refers to any computing system component that can operate independently. More specifically, it indicates a program that can execute without benefit of an operating system, or a turnkey computing system that can operate without association with any other computing system.

Tablet. A small digitizer made for use on a desk top or on a work surface next to a workstation. Often such digitizers are low-resolution and used solely to position a cursor on the graphics display screen of a workstation.

Turnkey System. A complete, integrated, and tested computing system. A system in which the vendor is responsible for producing, integrating, delivering, installing, testing, and maintaining all hardware and software components.

User Interface. Describes the mechanisms of interaction between the CAD/CAM system user and the system. These mechanisms consist primarily of prompts, menus, and other on-line messages that require some response from the operator. In the most general sense, it also refers to all ergonomic issues involved in the operation of a computing system.

Vector. 1. A directed quantity described by its magnitude and direction. Line segments are vectors described by 2 end points. 2. Decribes a cathode-ray tube on which graphic data are represented by lines drawn from point to point rather than by illumination of a series of contiguous positions, as is the case on raster cathode-ray tubes.

Workstation. An input/output device assigned to a CAD/CAM system operator from which he or she can access and operate all system software and peripherals. A workstation usually consists of a display screen, a keyboard, and a working surface. The workstation may also have limited intelligence, the result of microcomputer chips mounted inside the chassis.

Selected Bibliography

Books

Artist and Computer. R. Leavitt, ed., Harmony Books, One Park Avenue, New York, NY 10016. 1976.

CAD/CAM Computer Graphics: A Survey and Buyer's Guide. Charles M. Foundyller, ed., Daratech Inc., P.O. Box 410, Cambridge, MA 02238. 1982. A comprehensive listing of CAD/CAM systems, graphic workstations, application software, and peripheral devices.

The Complete Computer Graphics Management Anthology. Joel Orr, ed., Management Roundtable, Chesnut Hill, MA. 1981.

Computer-Aided Graphics and Design. D.L. Ryan, Marcel Dekker, Inc., 270 Madison Ave., New York, NY 10016. 1979.

Computer Graphics, CAD, and CAD/CAM Product Guide and Supplier's Directory. Interco Business Consultants Ltd., Frost and Sullivan Inc., eds., 106 Fulton St., New York, NY 10038. 1982. A 2-volume directory and purchasing guide to the entire international computer graphics industry.

The Computer Graphics Glossary. Stuart W. Hubbard, The Oryx Press, 2214 N. Central at Encanto, Phoenix, AZ 85004-1483. 1983. A comprehensive glossary of terms and product names pertinent to the computer graphics industry.

Computer Graphics Marketplace 1983-84. John Cosentino, ed., The Oryx Press, 2214 N. Central at Encanto, Phoenix, AZ 85004-1483. 1983. A comprehensive reference guide to the computer graphics industry including information about companies, products, professional organizations, services, educational programs, and conferences.

Digital Picture Processing. A. Rosenfeld and A.C. Kak, Academic Press, Inc., 111 Fifth Ave., New York, NY 10003. 1976.

Fundamentals of Interactive Color Graphics. James Foley and Andries van Dam, Addison-Wesley Publishing Co., Reading, MA 01867. 1980.

Geometric Principles and Procedures for Computer Graphics Applications. Sylvan Chasen, Prentice-Hall Inc., 521 5th Ave., New York, NY 10017. 1979. Outlines the primary geometric and analytic foundations upon which computer graphics applications are based.

Handbook of Graphic Presentation. C.F. Schmid and S.E. Schmid, John Wiley and Sons, Inc., 605 Third Ave., New York, NY 10158. 2d ed. 1979.

Harvard Library of Computer Graphics. Laboratory for Computer Graphics and Spatial Analysis, Harvard University Graduate School of Design, Gund Hall, Cambridge, MA 02138. Annual. A 17-volume set of technical articles and case studies on the computer graphics industry.

Introduction to Interactive Computer Graphics. J.E. Scott, John Wiley and Sons, Inc., 605 Third Ave., New York, NY 10158. 1982.

Management's Guide to Computer Integrated Manufacturing. John J. Allan III, Leading Edge Publishing, Inc., 11551 Forest Central Dr., Dallas, TX. 1981.

Raster Graphics Handbook. Conrac Corporation, Conrac Division, Covina, CA. 1980.

A Survey of CAD/CAM Systems. John J. Allan III, Leading Edge Publishing Inc., 11551 Forest Central Dr., Dallas, TX. 3rd ed. 1983.

Turnkey CAD/CAM Computer Graphics: A Survey and Buyer's Guide. Charles M. Foundyller, Daratech Association, P.O. Box 410, Cambridge, MA 02238. 1980.

Tutorial and Selected Readings in Interactive Computer Graphics. H. Freeman, ed., IEEE Computer Society, 10662 Los Vaqueros Circ., Los Alamitos, CA 90720. 1980.

Visual Display Terminals. A. Cakir, D.J. Hart, and T.F.M. Stewart; John Wiley and Sons, Inc., 605 Third Ave., New York, NY 10158. 1980.

Journals, Newsletters, and Proceedings

The Anderson Report. Anderson Publishing Co., Simi Valley Business Park, P.O. Box 3534, Simi Valley, CA 93063. A monthly publication reporting on recent developments in the CAD/CAM industry including industry analysis and editorials.

CAD/CAM Alert. Stewart Mawes, 822 Boylston St., Boston, MA 02167. A monthly publication that includes discussions of industry trends and reviews of new products.

Computer Graphics. "A Quarterly Report of SIGGRAPH-ACM" (Special Interest Group on Computer Graphics). Association for Computing Machinery, Inc., P.O. Box 12105, Church Street Station, New York 10249. A discussion of the latest technological developments in the computer graphics industry.

Computer Graphics World. PennWell Publishing Co., 1714 Stockton St., San Francisco, CA 94133. A monthly trade publication, devoted entirely to the computer graphics industry, which includes articles on applications, product developments, and industry business news.

Computers in Mechanical Engineering. American Society of Mechanical Engineers, United Engineering Center, 345 E. 47th St., New York 10017. A monthly journal that frequently publishes articles on computer-aided manufacturing applications.

Design Graphics World. Communication Channels, Inc., 6255 Barfield Rd., Atlanta, GA 30328. A monthly journal on the computer graphics industry featuring articles on the business as well the technology of graphics.

IEEE Computer Graphics and Applications. IEEE Computer Society, 10662 Los Vaqueros Circ., Los Alamitos, CA 90720. A bimonthly journal published in cooperation with the National Computer Graphics Association and dedicated to technical articles on computer graphics and CAD/CAM.

Machine Design. CAD/CAM Special Issue, Vol. 8, No. 25, November 8, 1984. Penton/IPC, Penton Plaza, Cleveland, OH. This issue is dedicated to a discussion of the newest developments within the CAD/CAM industry.

National Computer Graphics Association Proceedings. 2033 M St. N.W., Ste 330, Washington, DC 20036. Contains reprints of papers delivered at NCGA meetings, as well as discussions of recent technological developments in the computer graphics field.

The S. Klein Newsletter on Computer Graphics. S. Klein, 730 Boston Post Rd., Ste. 27, P.O. Box 392, Sudbury, MA 01776. A biweekly newsletter discussing the latest business and product development news in the computer graphics industry.

Special Interest Group on Computer Graphics (SIGGRAPH) Proceedings. Association for Computing Machinery, Inc., 1133 Avenue of the Americas, New York 10036. Discusses topics of interest to professionals working in computer graphics industry.

Index

Compiled by Linda Webster

Acceptance test, 96, 111, 113
Aeronautics industry, 24
Air traffic control, 2, 24, 63
Aliasing, 113
American National Standards Institute, 9
Antialiasing, 40, 68
Applications software, 22, 61–68, 109, 113. *See also* Software.
Applicon, 10, 25
Architecture and architects, 24, 52, 63, 73, 78, 94
Artificial intelligence, 5
Automation. *See* CAD/CAM
Automobile industry, 4
Auto-Trol Technology Corporation, 7, 10, 25, 52

Benchmark test, 62–63, 95–96, 108, 111, 113
Bidding procedures, 95–96, 107–12
Business graphics, xv, 63. *See also* Computer graphics.

CAD/CAM
  benefits, xvi–xvii, 12–28, 75–76, 78–81, 91
  company impact, 11, 91, 92
  costs, 27, 81–82
  definition, xiii, xv–xvi, 114
  drawbacks, 17–18
  evaluation, 84–85, 100–02
  failures, 77
  history, 1–10
  implementation, ix–xi, 92–96
  industry applications, 24, 63–64, 78
  justification, 89–91
  management issues, 72–73, 87–102
  management support, 89–92

  personnel requirements, 69–74
  planning, 18–19, 75, 77–79
  specifications, 108–09, 111
  standards, 8–9, 49–50
  statistics, 9
Calligraphic display devices, 31, 67. *See also* Display devices.
Calma, 7, 10, 25
Cameras, 44–45
Cathode-ray tubes, 30, 34, 114
Central processing unit, 30, 40, 114, 115
Clipping, 114
Color displays, 8, 32, 67, 103–05
Companies. *See* Vendors.
Computer drawing, 64–68
Computer graphics, 87–88. *See also* CAD/CAM.
  definition, F–G, 114
  history, xiv, 1–4, 87
Computer hardware, 6–9, 29–47. *See also* Mainframe computers; Minicomputers; Software; Turnkey systems; Workstations.
  16-bit systems, 7, 8
  specifications, 108–09, 111
  32-bit hardware, 7, 8
Computer-aided design. *See* CAD/CAM.
Computer-aided manufacturing. *See* CAD/CAM.
Computer-integrated manufacturing, 77
Computervision, 9, 25
Consultants, 71–72, 78, 81, 90
Control Data Corporation, 4
Coons, Steve, 4
CPUs, 30, 40, 114, 115
Creativity, xiv, 5, 12, 13
CRTs, 30, 34, 114

Cursor control devices, 35, 36–37. *See also* Input devices.

DAC-1, 4, 6
Daratech, Inc., 70
Data General, 7
Data processing, 114
Data processing departments, 88, 94
Data processing personnel, 70, 72, 88
Database management, xv, 21–22, 98–99
DEC. *See* Digital Equipment Corporation.
Design Augmented by Computer, 4
Design process, 9, 12–17, 22–24. *See also* CAD/CAM.
Designers, 52, 73, 88, 94, 95, 102
Digigraphics, 4
Digital devices, 45
Digital Equipment Corporation, 6–7
Digitizers, 37–38, 61, 114
Disk drives, 35, 46–47, 109
Disks, 45–46, 109
Display devices, 7–8, 29–35, 41, 115
Display techniques, 66–68
Distributed processing, 7, 115
Documentation, 15–16, 24, 110–11
Drafting and drafters, ix, xv, 9, 11, 12, 19–22, 35, 52, 63, 73, 78, 82, 88, 94, 95, 102. *See also* CAD/CAM.

Electroluminescence technology, 34
Electrostatic plotters, 44
Employees, 18–19, 57, 69–74, 79–80, 94–95
    motivations, 52–53, 65, 99
    training, 74–76, 95, 111
    workstations, 50–55
Engineering, ix, xiii, 22–23, 35, 63–64, 78
Engineering departments, 15, 88, 94
Engineers, 11–13, 19, 52, 73, 94, 95, 102
Ergonomics, 8, 49–55, 109, 115
Extrusion, 65

Film recorders, 44–45
Floppy disks, 46
Fractal geometry, 68
Function keys, 37, 115

General Electric, 25
General Motors, 4, 71
Gerber, 10
Graphics. *See* Business graphics; CAD/CAM; Computer graphics.

Graphics system software, 59–61, 109. *See also* Computer graphics; Software.
Group technology, xv, 12, 16–17, 80

Hardware. *See* Computer hardware.
Hidden lines, 66–67, 115

IBM, 6, 9, 25, 68
Icons, 61
Impact printers, 43–44. *See also* Printers.
Initial Graphics Exchange Specification, 9
Ink jet plotters, 3, 43. *See also* Plotters.
Input devices, 29, 30, 34–40, 98
Input techniques, 64–65
Interactivity, 2–3, 5, 6, 8, 115
Intergraph, 10, 25
Itek Laboratories, 4

Joystick, 30, 36, 37. *See also* Input devices.

Keyboard, 30, 34–35, 59, 60. *See also* Input devices.

Laser printers, 44. *See also* Printers.
Laser scanners, 45. *See also* Scanners.
Layering, 20, 116
Light pens, 3, 30, 35–37, 59, 60. *See also* Input devices.
Lighting, 50, 51
Liquid crystal display, 34
Lockheed-Georgia, 71
Lofting, 65

Machine tooling, xiii, 12, 17
Magnetic disks, 45–46
Magnetic tape drives, 46–47, 109
Mainframe computers, 88, 89, 93, 94
Maintenance, ix, x, 82, 83–84, 97, 101–02, 110
Management, 11, 69, 70, 71, 74, 78, 99
    of CAD/CAM operations, 72–73, 87–102
    preparation for CAD/CAM, 18–19, 24
    support for CAD/CAM, 89–92
Management information systems, 94
Mandelbrot, Benoit, 68
Manufacturing and Consulting Services, Inc., 41
Manufacturing processes, xiii, xvi–xvii, 12–17, 63. *See also* CAD/CAM.
Mapping industry, 65, 78

Massachusetts Institute of Technology, 2, 3, 4
McAuto, 10, 25
McDonnell-Douglas, 25
Megatek Corporation, 41
Memory, 32–33
Menu overlays, 38
Menu pads, 38–39
Microfilm photographic plotters, 2. *See also* Plotters.
Military applications, 2, 24, 64
Minicomputers, 7, 93, 94
Modeling systems, xiii, 4, 12, 16, 22–23, 65
Monitors, 30, 35. *See also* Display devices.
Motorola, 7
Mouse, 30, 36, 37. *See also* Input devices.
MV computers, 7

National Institute for Occupational Safety and Health, 50
National Semiconductor, 7
Navy, 71
Networking, 116
Noise, 50, 51
Nova computers, 7

Operating system software, 57–59, 109. *See also* Software.
Operators. *See* Employees.
Optical scanners, 39, 116. *See also* Scanners.
Oscilloscopes, 2
Output devices, 41–45, 109
Output requirements, 97–98

Patching, 65
PDP computers, 6–7
Pen plotters, 42–43. *See also* Plotters.
Peripheral devices, 2, 116
Personnel. *See* Employees.
Piping design, xiii, 22, 64, 78
Plasma displays, 33–34
Plotters, 2, 29, 42–44
Preventive maintenance. *See* Maintenance.
Prime, 10
Printers, 43–44
Productivity, 19–23, 50, 53–55, 65, 78, 81–82, 102
Programers, 73, 75

Raster display devices, 8, 32–33, 67, 117. *See also* Display devices.
Repair and maintenance. *See* Maintenance.
Request for proposal, 96, 107–12
Robotics, xiii, 17, 24
Rollerballs, 36, 37

Sales agreement, 96
Scanners, 39, 45, 116
Schlumberger, 25
Security systems, 99, 101
Service bureaus, 25–26, 93
Service contracts, 83–84. *See also* Maintenance; Vendors.
SIGGRAPH Graphical Kernel System, 9
SKETCHPAD system, 3–4, 24
Software, ix, 57–68
    command-driven, 59–61, 114
    dependability, 100–01
    design, 51, 53, 55
    documentation, 101
    menu-driven, 59–61, 116
    plotters, 43
    source code, 110–11
    specifications, 109, 111
    upgrades, 84, 110
Sony Corporation, 34
Sperry Univac computers, 7
Surface shading, 67
Sutherland, Ivan, 3
System analysts, 94

Tablets, 30, 35, 37, 61, 114
Texturing, 68
Thermal transfer printers, 44. *See also* Printers.
Thumbwheels, 36
Touchpads, 36
Trackballs, 36
Training, 74–76, 81, 82, 95, 111
Turnkey systems, 7, 25, 26, 93, 117

Upgrades, 82, 83, 84, 93, 101–02, 109, 110
User friendly, 51–52
User interface, 5–6, 117. *See also* Employees; Interactivity.

VAX computers, 7, 41
Vector displays, 8, 31–32

Vendors, 9–10, 25–26, 93, 94, 103
    benchmark test, 62–63, 95–96, 108,
        111, 113
    bidding procedures, 95–96, 107–12
    customer service, 83–84, 101–02,
        110
    marketing efforts, 94
    sales statistics, 9–10
    software, 84
    training programs, 74–75

VLSI chip technology, 41
Voice recognition systems, 39–40

Wharton School of Business, xiv
Winchester disk drives, 46
Word processing, 39
Workstations, 7–9, 29–35, 40–41, 46, 49–
    53, 66, 93, 103, 104, 109, 117

Xerox Corporation, 44